A Lutheran Primer
for Preaching

A Lutheran Primer for Preaching

A Theological and Practical Approach to Sermon Writing

Edward O. Grimenstein

CONCORDIA PUBLISHING HOUSE · SAINT LOUIS

Manufactured in the United States of America

4 5 6 7 8 9 10 11 12   24 23 22 21 20 19 18 17 16

Special thanks to Rev. Dr. Albert B. Collver for encouraging me to write this book.

Special gratitude to Bishop David Stechholz, English District, for being my first preacher.

Deep gratitude to Rev. Dr. Paul Scott Wilson for his graciousness in shaping young preachers into homileticians.

Deepest gratitude to my wife, Tevia, who displays the sacrificial love of Christ to our family every day.

CONTENTS

FOREWORD

"Just say the Word, Lord, and my servant will be healed."

— the Centurion (Matthew 8:8)

It is absolutely impossible to divorce the theological from the act of preaching. Over the past century, however, this has been the result in many churches. In many Western universities and seminaries, the "true" academic disciplines are seen as those that espouse the fields of exegesis or history or systematics, while regarding homiletics as the same rarely occurs. The act of preaching still retains a strong hold due to its place in public worship, but it is seldom engaged as a higher academic discipline. The end result of separating the act of preaching from the theological understanding of preaching has caused it to lose its moorings and has been a detriment to God's people and the Church, especially in the United States and Western Europe.

Today, homiletic texts are written with relatively no denominational significance. Homiletical texts are often viewed as being interchangeable from denomination to denomination, perhaps due to a lack of theologically distinctive homiletical texts. With moorings adrift, preaching has lost an understanding of its own significance in the life of the Church. The act of preaching has become a time for dramatic skits, moralistic engagement, telling stories, recounting fables and jokes and the like. It appears that the modern world has lost sight of what God does in preaching and the clergy themselves are unaware of what they should be doing through preaching.

It is one thing to say that preaching needs a reformation because indeed our sinful hearts should be daily drowned and washed. What preaching most desperately needs is a reattachment to the theological community of faith so that the preached Word is once again imbued with that special Word of God that invites people to believe and by believing have eternal life

(John 20:30–31).[1] God willing, the ultimate goal of this primer is to assist preachers in understanding the theology behind the act of preaching. Since people are indeed saved by hearing the Gospel, then such an act surely warrants sound theological and confessional pondering for improvement. Paul himself opined to the Roman congregations that people would be unable to believe without having someone preach.[2] Since such a gracious activity (i.e., believing) occurs through preaching by the Gospel of God Himself, then surely it warrants appropriate theological reflection.

The second goal of this primer is to provide students of preaching—new or experienced—the forum to discuss some of the necessities that should be considered in sermon writing. Although primers are typically reserved for beginning students of a discipline, this primer does have application for experienced preachers due to the deficit in preaching over the past few decades. For beginning students, it will provide a discussion of the steps taken to write an actual sermon by engaging a text, discovering the Law and Gospel in that text, identifying a theme and then writing the actual sermon. Although experienced preachers most certainly have their own prescribed methods for writing a sermon, it is always helpful to engage this unique task from other venues and vantage points.

The structure of this primer is designed in two sections. The first section concentrates on establishing a Lutheran theology for homiletics. The second section proposes more practical steps to encourage preachers in the actual writing of a Lutheran sermon. In order to foster engagement among students and professors, each chapter will conclude with questions that can be used in the classroom or as homework. These are written with the intent of having students, teachers and preachers engage in a sound theological discussion of what is accomplished by the preaching task.

Christ is not only still present in His Word as some mere medium or manner of content, but He Himself is bringing salvation into this world, as

---

1   The Gospel of John records, "But these are written so that you may believe that Jesus is the Christ, the Son of God, and that by believing you may have life in His name" (John 20:31 [ESV]).

2   "How then will they call on Him in whom they have not believed? And how are they to believe in Him of whom they have never heard? And how are they to hear without someone preaching?" (Romans 10:14 [ESV])

we believe God's Holy Word preached through the mouth of the pastor and, by believing, become possessors of eternal life.[3]

To God alone be the glory!
Edward Grimenstein
February 2015

---

3   Luther's Second Petition to the Lord's Prayer says, "How does God's kingdom come? God's kingdom comes when our heavenly Father gives us His Holy Spirit, so that by His grace we believe His holy Word and lead godly lives here in time and there in eternity" (Small Catechism, p. 20).

CHAPTER 1

BEGINNING A THEOLOGY OF THE WORD

"And God said . . ."

—Genesis 1

In the beginning, God created the world by speaking. He ordered things that did not exist to come into existence. He commanded things that were nothing to become something. He called out to things that were not and made them things that are. This is the proper beginning of not only understanding our story of salvation in God through His Son, Jesus Christ, on a cross, but this also shapes our understanding of how God speaks and how God still speaks today by means of a preacher.

Before undertaking a study of the Church's theology of the Word—and subsequent speaking of it—it is important to understand the nature of homiletical theology. Upon this proper understanding, preaching will either stand or fall. Perhaps the best place to begin in establishing a homiletical theology is creation. This is appropriate for two reasons. First, it is no coincidence that God created all of the cosmos by speaking. He could have chosen many different routes. He could have thought the cosmos into existence. He could have wiped His hands. He could have sneezed. Instead, God chose to speak. That was God's choice, not ours. And because of this fact, preaching has been inextricably linked to creation and will be until the end of time. Second, not only does God speak, but He speaks a creating Word. Speaking does nothing unless it is creating. Otherwise, speaking can be abusive, damning, or judging. God's Word is different though. His speaking is the building up of realities and states of existence that simply did not exist before that speaking.

In the Western world, speech is often considered a symbolic means of communication. This means that words are assigned to objects and those objects are manipulated via verbs, described by adjectives and the like. However, there is little discussion as to what words actually accomplish outside of the symbolic or representational approach.[1] Such an approach to language has directly affected preaching. Many Western sermons do not stress how language directly impacts listeners. Instead, there is a very strong emphasis upon more passive ways of reaching hearers. Although preaching has certainly been impacted by the general Western opinion regarding language, it has also been impacted by a very specific theology of preaching.

In 1971, the first publishing of Fred Craddock's increasingly popular *As One Without Authority* assisted in further emptying the authoritative claim God's Word has upon the lives of listeners.[2] Such a belief was the culmination of the Church's unique approach to Scripture during this period. Helpful here would be further explanation of Craddock's impact on preaching, which involved the viewing of Scripture as something that inherently lacked the power to make change in people's lives. Since the Scriptures were viewed as being normatively suspicious in the lives of hearers, then preachers would generally be unable to rely upon those Scriptures to be the bearer of that which would convert others. Since the Scriptures could no longer perform this task, people, such as Craddock and others, suggested a new way. This way, often referred to as the "new homiletic," essentially involved a move toward inductive approaches in preaching (like narrative) so that the hearer might become the final arbiter of God's Word.

The spoken Word of God tended to be viewed in higher critical terms which divorced that spoken Word from the re-creative nature inherent within the Word. But instead of reverting back to the Word in all of its transformative essence, homileticians like Craddock moved in the opposite direction and sought affirmation within man for the efficacy of God's Word and made man the final decider of that Word's re-creative nature. Good

---

1   There are some rhetoricians theologians who stand out as clear exceptions during the twentieth century, actually contributing a great deal to understanding language outside of non-representational speech. Some of these included Kenneth Burke's *The Rhetoric of Religion*, Gerhard Forde's *Theology Is for Proclamation*, John Searle's *Speech Acts*, and Paul Scott Wilson's *Four Pages of the Sermon* to name a few. Other than Gerhard Forde, there remains a lack of literature exploring this view of language from a homiletical perspective. Most do so from the field of rhetoric.

2   The greatest representation of this can be witnessed in the benchmark publication of *As One Without Authority* by Fred Craddock. At the time of its publication, this work represented a growing attitude in Europe for 50 years prior and also reflects the current trends in homiletics almost 50 years after its original publication.

intentions, but unfortunately such a practice drove preaching further away from the original essence of God's Word in Eden and once again tempted men with the fruit that they, too, may become gods.

Although Europe and the United States may have seen a general rise in viewing language as symbolic and representational, the words of Scripture still promote a very different approach to language. For example, in the Western world, words are generally accepted as neutral. Words represent items. They describe items or what items do. But in general, language is often viewed in symbolic terms. The word "cat" does not exist in and of itself. It only receives its meaning and understanding by the thing in reality to which it refers, namely, a small mammal with whiskers that meows.

Although the Scriptures certainly utilize symbolism and representation, there is a stark contrast from the very beginning. In Hebrew, the word for a "word" is *dabar*. This certainly does refer to a thing, but there is a greater nuance. Connected to the item is an action. There is inherently a doing. The Word is a doing by the One who is the Doer. This can be most easily seen in the creation account of Genesis. God, the Doer, spoke. And in speaking, the Doer did. This may seem simplistic to say. It may even appear confusing on the outset to identify. But the next few chapters will explore the very important theological implications of a Church that claims that there is truly only One Doer, who, by His very nature, can only do certain things. And in the doing of those things (preaching for one), the Doer (God) can perform for His people what He alone can do: save mankind from this fallen world. The next few chapters will build upon this current proposal and offer opportunities for discussion on the topic of representational versus active speech as the proper means to communicate the salvation for us accomplished in the person of Christ.

IN-CLASS ACTIVITIES / GROUP DISCUSSION

1. Read excerpts from Genesis 1, especially in Hebrew and Greek whenever possible (Gen. 1:1–28; John 1:1–18; 1 John 1:1–10). Take note and discuss those physical items that were brought into creation or existence through God's speaking.

2. Throughout the Gospel of John, Jesus makes seven "I am" statements. One statement was so offensive to the teachers of the law that they wanted to kill Jesus. Read John 8:48–59. Why did the Jews want to kill Jesus? Discuss together why the name "I AM" was so dangerous to take for oneself?

3. God is the only One who exists by Himself, having no help to achieve that created state from anyone else. The unknown name for God (YHWH) stems from the root of the verb *hayah / ehyeh*, which means "to be," "I will be," "I am," "exists" or "is." The Creator of all of creation called into existence other beings and made some of them in His image and in His likeness. What is the significance of that action?

4. Western language tends towards the figurative, referential or symbolic. A classic sense of this understanding within the Church is the age-old discussion of Christ's presence in the Lord's Supper. When Christ says, "This is my body," some denominations translate the Word "is" in a figurative or symbolic sense. Others, like The Lutheran Church, translate it literally to mean Christ's physical body is present alongside the bread. Even when we can't see that physical body or blood of Christ, we can rely upon the Words and promises of God that declare this to us. During the Divine Service, what are the ways that congregation members encounter items or words that could be interpreted either literally or symbolically and figuratively?

OUT-OF-CLASS DISCUSSIONS / ASSIGNMENTS

1. Preachers deal with items that could be taken symbolically or literally. Take, for example, Baptism. During this activity, the person being baptized is said to be reborn a child of God, have his or her sins washed away, be united to the body of Christ, become an heir of salvation and so on. For Lutherans, these are very real and tangible realities, but they are not ones always seen with eyes or touched with hands. How can preachers speak of these items so they are indeed seen with the eyes and touched with the hands?

2. Try to note at least ten other examples or instances in which a preacher may be addressed with so-called non-reality realities. Also note the instances when these realities encounter hearers within a sermon.

3. Lutherans believe these are very true realities bestowed upon us by God Himself and, as such, have wide implications for the individual believer and the rest of the congregation. How could a preacher preach upon these challenging scenarios so that congregation members might recognize them as realities bestowed upon them by God?

CHAPTER 2

THE FALL

"Did God really say?"

—the serpent (Genesis 3:1)

In the beginning, God created the heavens and the earth by speaking. Little has been written to discuss how physical reality is shaped by speaking. Speaking is not often connected to physical reality. It is often viewed as spiritual or ephemeral, at the very least, while creation is considered to be more concrete and touchable. But in order to delve into the act of preaching and how preachers are to preach, suitable time should be spent exploring the ramifications of preaching upon physical reality.

The serpent's first and greatest sacrilege against his Creator, aside from open rebellion, was deciding to take for himself what belongs alone to God. This included not only wanting honor and glory for himself, but also choosing to corrupt for his own use the other great action of God: speaking. The very fact that the serpent was speaking was an act of rebellion. He took what was reserved for God, namely the creative act via speech, and corrupted that for his own personal usage and gain. Just as it was by speaking that the heavens came into being, so also is it by means of speaking that creation became corrupted.[1]

---

1   For an excellent discussion that lays the groundwork for how the language of creation has been corrupted see Article I in the Epitome to the Formula of Concord, "For the devil can create no substance, but can only, in an accidental way—with God's consent— corrupt the substance created by God" (*Concordia: The Lutheran Confessions* [St. Louis: Concordia, 2006], p. 477). There is still no parallel though compared to what God does via His speaking of salvation and the devil's speaking of corruption. The two are not synonymous. Only God creates. As much as the devil tries to emulate God, he will continually fail. He cannot create any substance as God can but only, by God's permission, corrupt that which has been created.

To properly understand a distinctly Lutheran theology of the Word of God and to properly understand how preachers should preach, it is vital to know who our enemy is, especially the enemy who corrupted this world by means of a spoken word. The devil has his own theology of the word. Although "theology" is often used to refer to "God," who is generally named as the Triune God—Father, Son and Holy Spirit—the term "theology" could be used to describe simply any false "god." Martin Luther speaks of this very clearly to preachers in his Small Catechism when asked, "What is the First Commandment? We should fear, love and trust in God above all things."[2] Who is our God? All a preacher would need to do is ask, "What is that which we fear, love and trust in the most?" If the answer is not the Triune God as we survey the landscapes of our own hearts, minds and souls (and the hearts, minds and souls of our parishioners), then we have indeed found a false god whom we idolize.

This was Satan's plan from the very beginning. When Satan attacked Adam and Eve, he did not do so with a gun or an axe. Satan did not shout at them or call them names. He did not slither up and slap them in the face or punch them in their stomachs. Satan spoke. He attacked what they believed. He went straight to the heart of the true Christian theology of the Word and caused Adam and Eve to doubt what God had said. Satan brought unbelief into their souls by enticing them to doubt the promises of God. He brought despair into Adam and Eve's hearts by taking away from them the comfort they found in God's Word, crushing the promises they had in it and destroying the love they had for hearing it. Satan was an evil shepherd who called the sheep away from the pasture of their Good Shepherd and had them walk off a cliff. And he did all of this by speaking. No guns were fired, no fists were exchanged, no stones were thrown. Satan possessed a homiletical theology, and it worked.

Satan corrupted all of creation by having the ones made in the image of God fall into the same sin that he and a third of the angels embraced.[3] Satan enticed Adam and Eve not only to doubt God's Word— ripping the mat of faith from under their feet by having them doubt the veracity of it—but he also brought a false gospel of prosperity to them in which no harm would befall them. "You will not surely die. For God knows that when you eat of it your eyes will be opened, and you will be like God, knowing good and

---

2   Small Catechism, p. 11.

3   Revelation 12:4.

evil."[4] Satan preached a false good news to Adam and Eve that drew their eyes away from God and focused upon themselves. The fall into sin did not happen when Adam and Eve only ate the fruit. The eating sealed what had already happened in their hearts.[5] The fruit was confirmation of what they believed. The eating of the fruit was them signing on the dotted line that they had abandoned God forever and were now on their own.

The fall was comprised of primarily two elements. First, Satan spoke a false word. Second, Adam and Eve believed that false sermon. This was how the fall happened. No preacher in creation today can fully preach the true and right Gospel of Jesus Christ's salvation given freely to all of mankind without first understanding how the fall into sin happened. It happened when someone preached a false gospel and when people believed it. Lutheran preachers should look back into our Christian history as one looks through a rearview mirror while driving. It is good to look backward, while at the same time still move in a forward direction. We should not preach in such a way as Satan did. A Christian preacher should never preach so as to have man trust in himself again. That is not Christian preaching. That is satanic preaching. That is not a true gospel of Jesus Christ but is, instead, a false gospel. Such preaching will not save anyone; it will only confirm people's sins and confine them to everlasting hell. This is the challenge for modern-day preachers. We should know our history, but always do so while striving ahead, looking forward to the work of our Lord Jesus Christ.

---

4   Genesis 3:4–5 (ESV).

5   A correlation could be drawn between the eating of the Lord's Supper and believing as the "remedy" for the false believing and subsequent false eating that occurred in Eden.

In-Class Activities / Group Discussion

1. Read Gen. 2:4–25. What was the difference between how man was created and the rest of creation?

2. Read Gen. 3:1–7. How many times did the serpent speak to Eve?

3. Discuss what the serpent's objective was the first time he spoke to Eve. How did she respond? What phrase was added to Eve's response (see Gen. 2:17 for details)?

4. Discuss the serpent's second response in verse 4. Who did the serpent say that Eve could "be like"?

5. Discuss how the serpent's speech could be reminiscent of a sermon.

Out-of-Class Discussions / Assignments

1. Within the devil's sermon to Adam and Eve, he borrowed quite a bit that did not belong to himself. In what ways did the serpent corrupt God's Word in the content of his sermon? In what ways did the serpent corrupt God and man's unique ability tied to the creative, spoken Word?

2. The devil did not attack Adam and Eve with a gun or an axe. He spoke. Through this speaking he attacked what Adam and Eve actually believed. Study Luther's explanation of the First Commandment and its meaning. After the devil spoke with Adam and Eve, what was it that they believed they could become? What did Adam and Eve now fear, love and trust in most?

3. The devil's sermon was made up of primarily two elements: (1) a false gospel and (2) people who believed that false gospel. For Lutherans, we should be aware of this fact, but strive to preach the true Gospel and pray that people believe that Gospel. How does preaching and believing the true Gospel counter the work of Satan in our hearts, the Church and this world?

CHAPTER 3

RISING FROM THE FALL

"But say the Word, Lord . . ."

—the Centurion (Luke 7:7)

In the beginning, God created the heavens and the earth by speaking. Through the fall into sin, Satan corrupted what God had created by speaking a Word that pulled Adam and Eve's fear, love and trust in God away from their Creator and turned that devotion inward toward themselves. In the new creation of Jesus Christ, in which the Church now finds herself, the world is being changed again. This does not happen by manipulating the matter of creation. It does not happen through a political government's successes or through the social programs of this world. True change happens by speaking. But it is not just any speaking. Change occurs in the hearts and souls of people as a Word is spoken that turns peoples' fear, love and trust back to their Creator once more. This is the true Gospel.

The beginning of John's Gospel is unique and can rightly be said to set the stage for Lutheran preaching. John speaks very intentionally in the same language of Genesis. Genesis 1 begins by saying, "In the beginning, God created the heavens and the earth," while John's Gospel begins by saying, "In the beginning was the Word, and the Word was with God, and the Word was God. He was with God in the beginning . . . And the Word became flesh and dwelt among us" (John 1:1, 14).

The fall was not the greatest event in history. It could be argued that the greatest event, which even encompasses our salvation, is the incarnation of the Word—Jesus Christ—who took on our flesh. The Word became flesh.

Which Word? The Word that created creation, the Word that sustained Adam and Eve, the Word that lovingly banished them from the garden and made a true Gospel promise to them that the seed of the woman would

23

crush the serpent's head, the Word that came from Mt. Sinai, the Word that released and followed the people of God in the wilderness and sustained them in the temple and their synagogues, the Word had become realized in the incarnation of Christ. God's Gospel, His spoken Word of salvation, became a person. God became man. Out of His love for His creation, out of His mercy from His very nature, out of the One who loves the unlovable, He took on flesh to fulfill a plan set in motion before the creation of the world.

In Jesus Christ, the Good News that was promised in Eden and spoken throughout the Old Testament was now centralized and springing out from the man Jesus Christ Himself. John the Baptist had it right when he said to the crowds, "Listen to Him." John knew that this Jesus was the one who embodied within His flesh the spoken Word of salvation and that from Jesus a new Gospel would be spoken.

But what kind of speaking? This is the first stumble that many preachers mistakenly make today. Jesus spoke many things, enough that all the books in creation could not contain them.[1] And yet many lose sight of what that Gospel from Jesus is. Many groups will take Jesus' Words and speak them in such a way that they only provide a moral teaching to those who are listening. These teachings are neutral in and of themselves, and it is salutary for Christians to strive in ways that their heavenly Father sees as perfect in love toward God. However, preachers fall into Satan's trap when words stressing morality become a type of security blanket for the preacher and the hearers, as if acquiring a greater moral life somehow appeases God. This is a form of preaching that causes listeners to look inward to themselves for fear, love and trust, rather than looking to God. It is, by nature and definition, truly sinful and satanic.

Other preachers will make promises to people that if they live certain ways or if they only change their own minds and perspectives on life, then they can enjoy the fruits of this life and world and will be "successful." Such a teaching is also satanic, because it calls people to focus on the temporal benefits of this life and has nothing to do with having greater faith in Jesus as the Savior from their sin. For instance, although Jesus cares about the governments of this world, He is not seeking to support one political party or another. Jesus cares for the goods of this world and gives them to us, but He is not interested in having people gain a greater bounty in this dying, short life.

---

1   John 20.

That is to say, the greatest re-creation of the world is not necessarily in the physical world itself. The greatest re-creation, the one God truly desires, dwells within the unseen recesses of the hearts, souls and minds of people as they are invited to turn their glance away from themselves or others and instead to have trust in the One who created them and who is re-creating them through Jesus Christ.[2]

Preachers indeed have a challenging vocation. Amongst the many vocations given to men, aside from the vocations of fatherhood and motherhood, there is perhaps no greater vocation than to preach rightly in both the public forum of a congregation and in the home among the family. This vocation is intrinsic to the very personhood of man and could indeed even be as closely akin to men as gender has been ascribed to males and females.[3] And yet when it comes to men and women recognizing their God-given vocations as well as in preachers preaching the Word rightly, there will be challenges. As people with sinful natures, these tasks do not come naturally to us. Just as gender is staring people in the face as evidence of what by nature should be simply known (see Romans 3), so also proclaiming the Gospel of Christ should be a naturally occurring event between parents and children, neighbors with one another, and pastors to congregants. But that is simply not the case.

Due to the fall and the fact that no man can intrinsically from within his own nature know or speak the Gospel of himself, all preachers should be cautious and live not in fear of their task, but rather in humble acceptance and reverence toward the only One who can speak the Gospel: the Word

---

2   Lutheran preachers should be satisfied with Luther's words in the catechism: "How does God's kingdom come? God's kingdom comes when our heavenly Father gives us His Holy Spirit, so that by His grace we believe His holy word and lead godly lives here in time and there in eternity" (Small Catechism, p. 20).

3   In Romans chapter 1, Paul addresses the congregations with a logical argument. The movement begins with the Law and eventually moves them to a very free proclamation of the Gospel in chapter 3. What is unique though is that Paul begins with what should be normal and seen by all (i.e., gender of men and women and the subsequent shaming of genders through homosexual and other "shameless acts" in Romans 1:27). But from this appeal to natural knowledge to condemn the sin and their sinful state, Paul then moves the argument toward the Gospel. The Gospel is outside of and apart from man.

Himself, Jesus Christ.[4] There will be constant temptations for preachers to capitulate to the itching ears of some hearers, not to go too far in offending the sinner, in not going far enough in proclaiming the utter freeness of salvation. Preachers may even wrestle with some of the greatest temptations of laziness and lack of respect for the preaching task often manifested in poor preparation.

But preachers should also be aware of past history when it comes to the Word of God. They should be aware that mankind has lost the ability to know and understand what the Gospel is in ourselves, by ourselves and from ourselves.[5] And yet preachers should not despair. Through time spent preparing a sermon, speaking the sermon out loud and reflecting upon the theology of the Word, they can live in a state of constant repentance and renewal, just as every Christian is called to live. But preachers should never lose focus on the true Gospel, nor should true Christian preachers forfeit the Gospel and be tempted to speak another word that sounds good but, in fact, masquerades as a satanic word. Preachers should always remember that Satan pretends to be an angel of light.[6] This goes for preaching as well. There are many false preachers who preach "good" sounding words, words that are appealing to hearers or that may give people a worldly hope in a dying world. But these are not the true words of the One who is the Word: Jesus Christ.

---

4   The meaning to the Third Article of the Creed says, "I believe that I cannot by my own reason or strength believe in Jesus Christ, my Lord, or come to Him; but the Holy Spirit has called me by the Gospel, enlightened me with His gifts, sanctified and kept me in the true faith" (Small Catechism, p. 17). Preachers should never become despondent or weary in their task of preaching. Although it does not come naturally to men, Christ is the One who sustains all creation in His grace, including in the speaking of the Gospel.

5   Paul confirms this in Romans 3:10, 11 when he quotes Isaiah 52:5, "None is righteous, no, not one; no one understands; no one seeks for God" (ESV).

6   In 2 Corinthians 11:1–4, 14, Paul confirms the challenge the churches in Corinth are facing. The "super apostles" were coming and preaching a gospel other than the free Gospel of Christ and that just as the serpent deceived Eve by his cunning, so also would the Corinthians be led away from their "sincere and pure devotion to Christ."

In-Class Activities / Group Discussion

1. Read the account of the fall into sin in Genesis 3. Enumerate the instances in which proclamation (speech) is used to speak negatively of God.

2. Read the account of God proclaiming a curse in Genesis 3. Note who blamed who for the sin (i.e., Who did Adam blame? Who did Eve blame?). Did the serpent try to excuse his sin? Why would he be unrepentant and say nothing (John 8:44)?

3. Were Adam and Eve repentant for their sin? Why or why not?

4. Confession and Absolution is a time in which God speaks through the pastor to release people from their sin. What should first happen in Confession and Absolution (see Luther's Small Catechism)? Were Adam and Eve sorry for their sin or seeking release from their sin from God? Give clear examples to support your answer.

5. What was the first Gospel God spoke (i.e., in the words spoken to the serpent)? Was this promise of salvation from sin and death deserved or was it a gift?

OUT-OF-CLASS DISCUSSIONS / ASSIGNMENTS

1. Read Luther's Small Catechism on the Second Petition of the Lord's Prayer. Where is God's kingdom? How do we see God's kingdom in this world according to that petition?

2. How can the Gospel not only help bring God's kingdom into but actually become God's kingdom in this fallen world?

3. In what way does the Second Petition counter the sin in Eden and, in particular, the phrase, "so that by His grace we believe His holy Word . . ."? In what way was "believing" involved in the interaction between the serpent and Adam and Eve during their fall into sin?

4. What are some ways that fallen humans, ourselves included, can confuse God's kingdom in this life with other kingdoms of this world? How can preachers incorporate and center their sermons on "believing," as seen in and connected to the Second Petition)?

5. It is one thing to have people "believe" in Jesus, but preachers are often preaching to the congregation of saints who continue believing throughout their lives. What should a preacher consider when preaching to this type of congregation so that they may continue to believe and, as Scripture says, "by believing have eternal life"? (John 3:15).

6. What are some challenges that preachers may face and consider in preaching when it comes to God's kingdom in this world?

7. Read the Third Petition of the Lord's Prayer. How is God's will done in this world? How do we see God's will being done in this world according to that petition?

CHAPTER 4

A Trinitarian Approach to Preaching:

God the Father

"For there are three that testify . . ."

—1 John 5:7 (ESV)

Trinitarian Preaching

The previous section provided an approach to discuss a theology of preaching that is founded upon creation and the re-creation of the cosmos through Christ. As evidenced by Scripture, this creation and re-creation occurred through the speaking of the Word of God.[1] This Word of God is unique. It is a Word that called—from out of nothing—items to exist that had never before existed. A similar course could be taken to describe what happens in preaching and other forms of sacred speech inside and outside of worship: God calls faith, hope and love toward Him into existence within sinners. These are items that Lutherans believe, teach and confess did not exist before, but believe are called into existence by God.

---

1   See John 1; Genesis 1 and 3. Paul's references to preaching: particularly Romans 10:14; 1 Corinthians 9:18; Galatians 1:9. The number of passages referencing the positive impact of preaching within the Scriptures are far too numerous to recount. Regardless of the passage though, the intent is to see those passages that recount the re-creation of a fallen creation through Christ. This may or may not mention preaching particularly (as with some of the healing miracles of Jesus), but all involve the Word and all involve Christ.

The first step this primer took was to establish a theological approach to preach as a Lutheran. Now that central tenet will be expounded upon as we begin to shift from a theological discussion about preaching and move toward a theological approach to the actual practice of preaching. In order for any preacher to preach a sermon that is edifying to people, the Church and even Christ Himself, the preacher should not only know in an academic sense how the three persons of the Trinity are involved within the act of preaching, but also understand the involvement of the Trinity within the actual execution of the preaching act as the Gospel is spoken. This involvement is far more than merely a matter of content (e.g., when a sermon talks about Jesus as a person), but rather God the Father, Son and Holy Spirit's involvement in the preparation, writing and actual preaching of a sermon.

It should be noted that approaching the act of preaching from a Trinitarian perspective is far more than simply proposing a passing fad or gimmick. The field of homiletics, as with many academic institutions, is often saturated with new ways to approach old disciplines.[2] Approaching the act of preaching from a Trinitarian perspective is beyond a mere device. There is no formula, no gimmick. Rather, it would be best to describe this approach as a theological movement. Although this section will not yet advocate how to research, write, outline or deliver a sermon, nevertheless it will assist preachers with a proper approach to these tasks and begin to advance a distinctly Lutheran, homiletical theology toward its ultimate and proper goal of proclaiming Law and Gospel.

GOD THE FATHER

It may seem like a proverbial "no brainer" to propose that God should be a part of the sermon. If asked whether or not God was present and active in the sermon writing and preaching process, most preachers would probably respond with a resounding "Yes!" However, they might be hard pressed to advance that discussion. Most preachers would respond in this way because they would not want to say that an omnipresent God could in some way be absent from an event. But most preachers would probably be challenged to explain *how* God is active within the sermon. Most may give a somewhat

---

2   Eugene Lowry in *The Homiletical Plot* suggests that sermons should take a form in which the Gospel is relatively short at the end of the sermon and almost always a surprise. Paul Wilson in *Four Pages of the Sermon* proposes that sermons follow a metaphorical four-page setup corresponding to trouble and grace.

nebulous response, saying that God works through the sermon or is present in some mystical way, but otherwise there is nothing concrete to point a preacher's fingers at, allowing them to say, "This is God" or "This is where God is acting." But God chooses not to remain nebulous or mystical, nor is He absent from creation. God the Father instead chooses to be with His creation.

To say that God is "active" in the sermon is a bit of a misnomer. God is not merely active, but He can be, should be and actually is the primary actor within a sermon. However, just as with the fall, Satan can so corrupt the preacher that God is not allowed an active place within the act of preaching.

Most preachers unknowingly fall into the sin of relegating God to the backseat in the preaching act. At most, God becomes mere content within a sermon rather than the One who is truly doing the preaching. Most sermons will mention God. They will talk about God, or they will even refer to something God did in the Scriptures. But it is one thing to talk about God, and it is another thing altogether to allow God to be the One who is acting within preaching.

The best way to understand the active role God can and should play in the act of preaching can be found in the liturgy of the Divine Service. On a relatively passive level, it is easy to see the ways in which God is present within the service. Any person could walk into a Divine Service and see paintings of Christ on the walls, the Lord's Supper set on the altar or stained glass with different pictures of Scripture stories. And yet on a more direct and active level, there are instances in which God is clearly the primary acting agent within worship. This is not to say that God is not so in other instances, but simply that, in some cases, it is a very active and direct role.

In fact, the greatest active role that God has in worship is when God Himself is speaking. This should not be taken in some type of metaphorical or symbolic sense. Preachers should not be shy in saying that God truly does speak in worship. For example, many worship services begin with Confession and Absolution. Generally, there are two types of absolution that can be bestowed upon the congregation. One is considered to be a declaration of grace. In this, the preacher speaks words of comfort and reassurance to the congregation. They are reminded of the nature of God and, in that nature, they are to find reassurance that He forgives their sins.

However, declaring grace, or talking about grace, is something very different than actually giving that grace. For example, it is one thing to talk about forgiveness, and another thing actually to be forgiven. A true Absolution is one in which sins are actually, really and truly forgiven. This type of Absolution given to the congregation is generally considered to be the Word of God Himself. This can be argued by the fact that the pastor is the one standing in the stead of God Himself:

> Upon this your confession, I, by virtue of my office, as a called and ordained servant of the Word, announce the grace of God unto all of you, and in the stead and by the command of my Lord Jesus Christ I forgive you all your sins in the Name of the Father and of the Son and of the Holy Spirit.[3]

During this point in worship, God is the One who not only speaks as the actor for His people, but He is also the One doing the action by providing forgiveness. Such speech should never be considered as some type of flowery ornamentation of something greater somewhere else. The Absolution is the very thing itself. There is no reference. There is no symbol. There is no other meaning. It simply is. Through the Word of God an action occurs, and sins are forgiven.

It is this instance of God's activity that can and should be reclaimed within preaching and that is very often absent in modern homiletics. Thankfully, the Church has liturgical, hymnal and scriptural precedence for such activity. Consider for a moment Nathan confronting King David regarding his infidelity (2 Sam. 12:1). Nathan did not send himself. The Scriptures say that God sent him (2 Sam. 12:1). In such a moment, Nathan needed much more than his meager self in speaking to the king. He needed to have the King of kings and the Lord of lords on his side and, through the spoken Word, God was. God was active in speaking His own Word through Law and Gospel to David

Likewise, this quality of activity should be present in modern preaching. There is absolutely nothing wrong with the preacher of God actually speaking in a quote as if God Himself were speaking. The Gospel is antithetical to natural man. It does not reside nor originate from within natural man. The Gospel resides and originates only from God. In days gone by, this was widely and easily understood in preaching, and preachers often spoke in the

---

3 *Lutheran Service Book* (St. Louis: Concordia, 2006), p. 185.

literal first person, in the stead of God.[4] It was normative that the preacher spoke God's Word and spoke on behalf of God. There are many reasons why there could be challenges for this practice, but it is possible to do so in such a way that God can speak Law and Gospel to His people out of love and care for them.[5] There can also be no more powerful Word in the world than having God Himself speak the condemning Law and also the healing balm of the Gospel.

Imagine the power of such activity on Ash Wednesday when God pronounces, "How disappointed I am. How grieved I am that you have left Me." Or imagine the great consoling comfort when such a practice could be engaged rightly during a funeral. There is nothing stronger in this world than to know that God Himself is for us and acting on our side when He says, "I told you I would never leave you. I told you I would never forsake you. I wasn't kidding. I wasn't lying. That's why I had David write, 'Even though I walk through the valley of the shadow of death, I will fear no evil.' I meant what I said. I won't leave you." God has always been present with His people, and God is and will still be with His people through His spoken and preached Word.

---

4   Luther himself used this convention quite often throughout his preaching. In fact, it was a relatively common occurrence for him to speak on behalf of the congregation, devil and even God (*Luther's Works* [Philadelphia: Fortress Press, 1959], 51:29).

5   Ever since the publication of Fred Craddock's *As One Without Authority*, there have been challenges regarding the authority that preachers might utilize when preaching.

In-Class Activities / Group Discussion

1. How is God the Father active in the sermon?

2. Is His activity more in content (like a noun) or more in doing (like a verb)? What about both?

3. What are some of the challenges modern preachers face when considering God's activity in the sermon?

4. What parts of the liturgy can provide a template for preachers to better understand how God acts through words?

5. Review the Absolution, Words of Distribution, baptismal rite and other portions of the liturgy. How does God speak through these pieces to the congregation?

Out-of-Class Discussions / Assignments

1. Review those parts of the liturgy where God speaks directly to the congregation (Absolution, Lord's Supper, hymns, readings, etc.). Select a portion of a current sermon where the Gospel is proclaimed. Identify a small excerpt, and try to rewrite the Gospel proclamation as a direct quote, keeping to about one sentence in length. Share with the group, class or instructor for feedback.

2. Select a portion of a sermon (either the same as above or new) in which the Gospel was proclaimed. Now expand this proclamation into a full paragraph.

3. Repeat the same exercise above, this time creating a paragraph that possesses both Law and Gospel.

CHAPTER 5

A Trinitarian Approach
to Preaching:

God the Son

Within the act of preaching, there is no doubt the actor should be God Himself. But what exactly should that preaching entail? When asked, many preachers would probably confess that they preach, as Paul said, Jesus Christ crucified.[1] Undoubtedly, there are many opinions as to what it means to preach Jesus. Higher criticism, for instance, has had a profound effect on preaching. In particular, it impacted how a theologian is to interact with Scripture and how the theologian should regard Scripture. But one of the most poignant—and detrimental to the Church—impacts is that higher criticism encouraged theologians, pastors and congregational members to become "masters" of the Word read, studied and preached. It is questionable how and if the Western Church will recover its vitality from this theological malady.

As an academic tool, higher criticism provided the Church more of a scalpel than a chisel. It tended to engage a biblical topic along the lines of tearing it apart to discover its riches, rather than allowing the structure of Scripture to stand on its own and to learn from it. The Word of God ceased to have an element of awe, wonder and innate authority. The Scriptures could now be taken apart and studied, rearranged into new figures and patterns depending upon the will of the man who subjected them to such frustration (i.e. sinful man).

---

1   1 Corinthians 1:23.

With regard to preaching in particular, however, the most dramatic loss was loss of the belief that God not only came to us in the spoken Word of the Scriptures, but that Jesus Christ still acts toward His creation via the preached Word. A dissected word cannot act. A torn apart word has no ability to function. A broken word does not have power to move. But that is not the Word of God!

God chose to act toward this creation through the spoken Word. That was God's choice, not ours. We see this throughout the Scriptures: God created the heavens and the earth by speaking. Satan tempted Adam and Eve not just with a physical element but by means of speaking, becoming the first liar and murderer by corrupting God's Word. Jesus Himself declared that as the Word He would be taking on our flesh to rescue us and, indeed, He did that very thing. Now, during the present ministry of the Church following Christ's ascension we are still speaking and through that speaking, people are saved from their sins and given eternal life.

Jesus Christ is still speaking in this world. There is certainly a place for understanding the grammatical structure of words and understanding the rules of grammar and logic in order to promote the faith. However, that should not be the ultimate goal of understanding the Scriptures. The Bible should not only point to Jesus Christ but also be His own Words that He is speaking to creation, while the ultimate goal remains strengthening one's faith in Jesus as the Church's Savior, Lord and Groom. The Scriptures and preaching should not only point toward Jesus as a manner of content,[2] but they should also be seen as the present, living, active voice of God Himself who is doing salvation amongst people in this world today, tomorrow and every day until the return of Christ Himself.

The greatest examples of such speaking can be found in the historic divine liturgy. Portions such as the Absolution are excellent examples that highlight how the spoken Word cannot be dissected or explained away. The Word is not parsed out or discussed in a Bible study. The Word is not rewritten so that the Scriptures talk about salvation as a thing rather than allowing the spoken Word to actually grant salvation. For example, it is one matter

---

2   It is very common when surveying modern sermons to see Jesus described by means of content. The name "Jesus" will appear in the sermon but only as a point of reference, in the same way that a homeowner, when touring their home for visitors, might point to a curio on a shelf and say, "Oh, and that is a ceramic piece I bought while in Italy, now let's move on to the upstairs . . . " Jesus is often referred to in sermons as a thing that might as well be sitting upon a shelf.

to talk about oxygen as a thing and quite something altogether different to actually breathe the oxygen. Preaching needs to allow hearers to breathe.

When, in the words of the Absolution, the pastor says, "I forgive you all of your sins," the pastor, congregation, saints in heaven and even God Himself are standing in the front row, watching the new creation being rebuilt in that exact moment. Creation was made by God speaking, and it was corrupted by Satan speaking a corrupted word.

Jesus spoke and became the Word in flesh. Now He is re-creating this world He loves so much in the same way He created it in the first place: by speaking. Consider the following sermon based on the reading of the healing of the ten lepers (Luke 17:11–19). The first is a poor example of Christ being present, while the second highlights how Christ desires to be active in preaching:

> Only one of the lepers went back to Jesus. He brought thanks to Jesus, and Jesus applauded him for being the only one. That is often the case in our lives. We receive blessing from Jesus, and we don't offer thanks. We don't pray. We don't attend church. Instead, it is like we just take our blessing and run. We really should give thanks more.

The above example is terrible for multiple reasons. First, the passage has been misinterpreted. Instead of concentrating upon Jesus, the preacher has concentrated upon the leper. This results from failing to interpret the text rightly, rather than noting where Gospel lies and concentrating upon it in the sermon.

Second, the Law is emphasized in this passage rather than the Gospel in Christ. Ask yourself, "Who is doing the action in this sermon?" The answer is simple: us. The sermon concentrates upon us and what we have done or have not done. Indeed, the sermon could almost end by saying, "Make sure you pray more."

Third, the greatest offense is in regard to Jesus. Review that example and ask, "What is Jesus doing in this passage?" The answer: absolutely nothing! Jesus might as well not even be there. He is just mentioned in the Bible verse. He is not active nor is He doing anything in the present, a not-so-subtle way of denying His resurrection. This is an example of how Jesus can remain inactive, sitting on the preacher's proverbial shelf like a cute little knick-knack.

The second example is quite different:

> The Samaritan learns and knows that the only guy who can help him is Jesus. Jesus gives healing. Jesus gives life. The only conclusion faith can make is that you need to be where Jesus is. Where Jesus is, there is life. The Samaritan knows that Jesus has more gifts. He clings to Jesus . . . He [Jesus] baptized you, marking you as God's own child. He absolves you over and over, and He feeds you with the never-ending feast of His body and blood for your salvation. That's not just for when you are in trouble, when things aren't working right, when things aren't going your way, when you need a shot of "pick me up" from Jesus. His gifts are for you always unto eternal life. His gifts are not just one-shot deals but a continually flowing spring of forgiveness, life and salvation.[3]

The former example faced many challenges, but the latter is almost the polar opposite. First, this passage is interpreted correctly with an emphasis upon God rather than upon the leper or Samaritan. The Samaritan has a place, but it is one that is at the feet of His God. Second, the Gospel is emphasized in this passage as opposed to the Law. There is no calling for the individual to do something to better his life or improve his condition. Instead, the hearer is directed toward the only One who brings salvation: God in Christ. Finally, the greatest difference is in relation to Jesus. While the first passage placed Jesus up on a shelf and gave Him a useless role in the sermon, this passage places Jesus front and center in the sermon. Notice the verbs related to what Jesus is doing. Jesus is described as the One who "baptized you, marking you as God's own child. He also "absolved you over and over." He "feeds you with the never-ending feast of His body and blood." Jesus is the central figure to this sermon, and He is doing great, wonderful and eternal things for the hearer, just as He promises to do.

The greatest challenge modern preachers will face in their preaching is the challenge of allowing Jesus to speak in the sermon. I do not mean to imply the addition of a greater number of Bible quotes, nor would this entail some type of tomfoolery of contemporary tricks to make it look like Jesus is more present through the use of extended metaphors or similes. He is not present by means of a well-formed argument, nor should the preacher jump to the

---

3   Sermon excerpt is from a 2013 Thanksgiving Day sermon from Rev. Michael Kumm, preached at Trinity Lutheran Church in Millstadt, Illinois.

proverbial head of the line by dressing up like Jesus while somehow hitting people over the heads with a dramatic performance of false incarnation.

Having Jesus speak in the sermon means something far different and takes time to consider, ponder through good pastoral reflection and discussion, and then enact in practice. Changes to our theology of worship should indeed come slowly and deliberately through counsel among fellow pastors. The end result would be one that allows Jesus to be the actor and the bringer of salvation and comfort in all preaching. This would mean that the practices in higher criticism that bottle Jesus up and place Him on a nice shelf, pulled down to use at a preacher's convenience, would cease. Jesus would also stop being a mere teacher of morals. He would no longer be regarded as the mere content of exegesis or the one who automatically nods in capitulation to anything the preacher wants. Higher criticism's effects on preaching are dangerous to the efficacy of the preached Word. Perhaps the greatest sin of the twentieth century is that such oppositions to Christ were permitted to infiltrate the Christian Church unabated. Systematics may have guarded the front door, but poor preaching slid in through the back.

Christ's desire is to bring salvation to this world and to release this world from the grip of its sinful condition. This release is being offered to all of creation through the speaking of a Word. This desire to save creation through the spoken Word can be seen clearly through the story of the centurion who came to Jesus asking for healing.[4] Jesus was willing to go to the home and heal the servant, but the centurion requested that Jesus only speak the Word. The centurion knew, and believed, that Jesus' Word was authoritative, because Jesus Himself possessed authority. By that authority and by His command, it was unnecessary for Jesus to actually visit the sick servant. His Word would be enough. His Word would accomplish what it says it would accomplish. The Word was enough.[5]

---

4   Matthew 8:5–13.

5   "For Luther . . . Christian preaching—when it is faithful to the word of God in the Scriptures about our need and God's response to it—is God speaking. When it focuses on what God has done for the world in Jesus Christ, it is God speaking. When it invites faith and presents Christ so that faith becomes possible, it is God speaking. It is God's very own audible address to all who hear it, just as surely as if Christ himself had spoken it" (Fred Meuser, *Luther the Preacher* [Minneapolis: Augsburg Publishing House, 1983], 12).

This is the true nature of Jesus Himself who exists from eternity as the Word made flesh.[6] He is the One who not only was with God in the beginning, but in His very nature is the Holy One who acts by means of His spoken Word to create and, now in this present age, re-create this world through the forgiveness of our sins. What Jesus offers is a very real release from sin, death and the power of the devil. This occurs by allowing the preacher to speak the Scriptures and to preach his sermon in such a way that allows Jesus Himself to be present, living and active through those Words. As Luther said, "Through this office of preaching and of forgiving sins, souls are resurrected here from sins and from death."[7]

---

6   Both Gerhard Forde and Herman Stuempfle note Luther's emphasis that the Gospel is inherently God's actions directed toward people. Forde notes God's actions stressed in Luther by emphasizing the antithesis between sin and grace. See Gerhard Forde, *Theology Is for Proclamation* (Minneapolis: Fortress Press, 1990), 85, while Stuempfle notes God's actions stressed in Luther by means of God revealing Himself through the two different modes of Law and Gospel. See Herman Stuempfle, *Preaching Law and Gospel* (Ramsey: Sigler Press, 1990), 17.

7   Martin Luther, *Word and Sacrament II* (Philadelphia: Augsburg Fortress Press, 1959), 35.

In-Class Activities / Group Discussion

1. Discuss some of the challenges that higher criticism has placed upon the preacher's view of Scripture and even his own preaching.

2. How has higher criticism encouraged a preacher to view Scripture?

3. How has higher criticism encouraged a preacher to view Jesus during preaching?

4. How is Jesus, God the Son, present in preaching?

5. What is a continual challenge we fallen preachers face in this world when it comes to Jesus? How can Jesus be spoken so that He does not remain distant or past tense?

Out-of-Class Discussions / Assignments

1. Have the instructor (or students may look at previous sermon examples of their own) identify passages that speak of Jesus in the past tense, in a distant manner, or as inactive or passive. Share these in class. Now rewrite the same passage so that Jesus is present tense, close and active.

2. Read Luther's Small Catechism on Baptism and "What benefits does Baptism give?" What are the things that Baptism actually accomplishes?

3. Read the section on the Lord's Supper. What does the Lord's Supper really give us?

4. If Baptism and the Lord's Supper really can do such things, share the very real and sure things preaching does for the people of God.

5. How can Jesus be spoken so that He does not remain distant or past tense?

CHAPTER 6

A Trinitarian Approach
to Preaching:

God the Holy Spirit

Through the spoken Word of preaching, fallen creation comes face-to-face with Jesus Christ who, by His very nature, longs to redeem this creation and has done so through His death and resurrection. This is now given to people not only through Baptism and the Lord's Supper but continually by speaking a word of release to the "captives" in this world through preachers and Christians. Jesus does not do that by just talking about salvation as a thing, nor does He do this by dissecting the meaning of salvation and so destroying the thing itself. Jesus does not keep Himself high and out of reach so that salvation can only be pondered as a far-off thing that cannot be grasped by ordinary people.

As the Scriptures say, not only does faith "come by hearing,"[1] but also something very real and tangible happens in the present moment in creation (which could be quite to the chagrin of those who espouse the central tenets of higher criticism). Jesus' Words remain in many circles a Word that can still be spoken in such a way that permits Jesus to be who Jesus is: the bringer of salvation so that those who hear His Words of release might

---

1 Romans 10:17, "So faith comes from hearing, and hearing through the word of Christ" (ESV).

have the opportunity to be possessors themselves of that salvation and, by believing, already possess salvation here and now.[2]

It is very easy for pastors to get caught up in the myriad of voices connected to theology and preaching. Those voices and the general noise of this fallen world make it easy to forget a very simple premise: the Gospel is for you, the hearer. The angels announced this great work of Christ by saying to the shepherds, "For unto you is born this day in the city of David a Savior, who is Christ the Lord" (Luke 2:11 [ESV]). God chose speaking to be His means of creating and redeeming salvation. By means of the very act itself, Jesus reveals His love for creation and for each individual within that creation.

On a very basic level, any form of speech requires two things: a speaker who speaks and a listener who receives what was spoken. From the dawn of time to the end of days, God has set up nature itself and the salvation that comes to us to flow according to this pattern of speaking and listening. He does so in such a way that people will receive salvation by hearing the Word spoken to them and, by hearing, take that very Word into themselves and become possessors of that Word.

The Holy Spirit is the great comforter.[3] He chooses not to speak of Himself but is satisfied in pointing to the One who redeems creation right here and now. The purpose of this is accomplished in a very simple way: by believing. The Small Catechism says, "I believe that I cannot by my own reason or strength believe in Jesus Christ, my Lord, or come to Him; but the Holy Spirit has called me by the Gospel, enlightened me with His gifts, sanctified and kept me in the true faith."[4] The Holy Spirit causes people to believe. That believing begins by hearing God's Word spoken to people who long to hear that Word.

---

2   Luther says, "The chief article and foundation of the gospel is that before you take Christ as an example, you accept and recognize him as a gift, as a present that God has given you and that is your own. This means that when you see or hear of Christ doing or suffering something, you do not doubt that Christ himself, with his deeds and suffering, belong to you. On this you may depend as surely as if you had done it yourself; indeed as if you were Christ himself" (Richard Lischer, *Theories of Preaching* [Durham: The Labyrinth Press, 1987], 95).

3   "But the Helper, the Holy Spirit, whom the Father will send in My name, He will teach you all things and bring to your remembrance all that I have said to you" (John 14:26 [ESV]).

4   Small Catechism, p. 17.

Preaching is the means by which this occurs. As Luther said, "Through this office of preaching and of forgiving sins, souls are resurrected here from sins and from death."[5] When people hear that the Gospel is for them, when they believe that the Gospel is for them, when the preacher allows them the opportunity to see this, faith can occur. That is why the office of preaching should never be seen as insignificant, and a preacher's words must never be downplayed as having little effect. Preachers themselves should never treat their words in a frivolous manner, but show them the highest care, because it is by means of speaking that the world was created.

It is by speaking that the world is re-created through Christ. Through this verbal re-creation, God is declaring His creation to be new and remade. Even though sin shall remain, even though painful memories will still hold sway, even though death will be the unnatural end of all men, through preaching people are declared new persons through Christ. Through the Holy Spirit, people believe and are reborn in Him.

Luther said, "It is God who names or calls, and what he names immediately comes into existence."[6] A truly Trinitarian form of preaching not only allows God to be the actor and the Son to be the One who is bringing the action of salvation, but it is the Holy Spirit who appropriates that belief for persons. Although it is possible to believe in an object or a thing as a static, physical reality, believing has a different connotation.[7] Believing, when it comes to Christian faith, inherently means to believe in someone. Believing means to trust that particular someone will do what he or she has promised to do. In the case of salvation, it is in the work of Jesus Christ, our Lord. It means to believe in the One who has made us new in Christ. And it means to believe that we ourselves are indeed new people because God has claimed that we are. There is no other reason. God calls into existence, and what He calls automatically exists.

In the Old Testament, God was known as the Lord (YHWH). The unspeakable name of God took its root in a verb that was later translated in the New Testament as "I am" and was the name Jesus not only claimed for

---

5   Luther, *Word and Sacrament II*, 299.

6   Martin Luther, "This Is My Body" in *Word and Sacrament III* (Philadelphia: Augsburg Fortress Press, 1961), 117.

7   In response to the fanatics, Luther said, "It is a natural way of speaking that when someone points to a thing, we know what he is saying" (Luther, *Word and Sacrament II*, 337).

Himself but that almost got Him stoned.[8] What is important for preachers to remember is that God Himself is the only One who can claim existence for Himself. He is the only One who exists in and of Himself in creation. He does not need air to breathe or ground to walk on. He does not need the light of the sun by day or the moon by night. He does not need the gravity of the earth to survive or the warmth from a particular sun to stay warm. He is God. He exists in and of Himself. And as such, He is the only One who has authority to declare that we are new persons in Christ. God is the only One who can claim a new existence for us who rely upon the gravity of the earth to walk and the sun to warm and the air to breathe. God the Father, Son and Holy Spirit is the only One who can claim to us sinful persons that we are new persons. The One who exists is the only One capable of calling others into a new existence. He is the only One who can call us by a new name, the only One who can declare that we are a new people, the only One who can name us sinners as saints. By that naming, what He has called immediately comes into existence.[9] Through preaching, this naming happens. Through preaching, sinners don't just know they are a new creation, but they can believe they are a new creation, that they really are saints.

Preaching Jesus Christ and Him crucified literally has the ability to transform lives. When people hear and believe that they are new creatures, they become new creatures in Christ. Through this type of preaching, the type that invites people to believe in Christ as their salvation, their belief gains a surety as well as certainty that may not have come before because it may not have been offered before. People cannot believe unless they hear, and what they hear and how they hear it can make all the difference in the world. This certainty comes when people can believe without a shadow of a doubt that all of Christ's deeds and sufferings were done in their place and that those deeds and sufferings do indeed belong to them. Jesus did not suffer, die and rise again for His own sake. He did it for your sake. And it is for you, the listener, that preaching must ultimately appeal because Christ becomes very dissatisfied when His gift of eternal life is squandered and not shared in its full potency and vitality.[10]

---

8   See John 8:58.

9   Luther, *Word and Sacrament II*, 299.

10 See Revelation 3:15 and the condemnation Christ lays upon the congregation in Laodicea for being neither cold nor hot.

In the Garden of Eden, Satan lied to Adam and Eve. He had them believe that God's Word was not efficacious enough. He had them believe that they could look to themselves for freedom and life. The devil, Adam and Eve were wrong for believing this. But now Christ is calling us to look toward Him and, once more, to have mankind look toward His sufferings and death in such a way that we do not doubt that Christ Himself, with His deeds and suffering, belongs to us. In that moment of believing, Satan's lie is burst, and the new Adam in each of us turns away from Himself and looks toward the tree of eternal life in the cross, ripe with the fruit of Christ's body and blood. Upon that Christ all persons are nourished so that each of us may live in the new creation forever.

This is what preaching does. It does not merely talk about or discuss Christ. Preaching takes our hands, guides us to the cross, turns our heads toward Jesus and invites us to receive everything He has done for us. Good preaching invites us to find rest for our souls in Him and not in ourselves. Good preaching encourages us to eat and be satisfied in Him and not in the works of self. Satan does not want us to believe that Christ's death and resurrection are for "you." Satan will do absolutely anything to steal this away from Christ's Church. But let him try. Christ will never relent in speaking His Gospel through His servants in all times of persecution and famine, nakedness or sword.[11] In that speaking, and especially in that Trinitarian form of speaking, people will believe by means of the Holy Spirit who calls us to believe Christ's Word. The Holy Spirit instills once more within our hearts, minds and souls the belief we abandoned in Eden: faith in God. The God who first created creation loves it so much that He would never abandon it and is right now redeeming His creation until the end of time.

---

11 Romans 8:35.

In-Class Activities / Group Discussion

1. Why is it easy to forget some premises in preaching (e.g., that the Gospel is "for you")?

2. According to the meaning of the Third Article of the Creed, what is the main role of the Holy Spirit when it comes to people hearing the Word of God?

3. How is God's existence the fount from which our new existence in Christ flows?

4. What does Satan not want you to believe?

Out-of-Class Discussions / Assignments

1. Look through sermons you have preached before or sermons you have heard. When are the times when a preacher has said to the congregation that preaching is "for you"?

2. What are the ways the preacher might speak the Word so that hearers might have the chance to hear and ultimately believe in Jesus?

3. Through preaching, God declares people are a new creation in Christ, and by His declaration, we are new creatures in Christ. Take note of those instances in preaching where such a declaration occurs and share them in class.

CHAPTER 7

Preaching Law to Gospel

"The righteousness of God has been manifested."

—Romans 3:21 (ESV)

It is one thing for preachers to consider simply the manner of content that is preached. Preaching is not a matter of merely plugging in the right words into the right form. Neither is preaching a nebulous, mystical experience in which a preacher may simply babble. The true concern of preaching is believing. The question preachers should be concerned about is whether or not their preaching is allowing people the opportunity to believe that Jesus is the Christ and, by believing, have eternal life.[1] This believing does not happen simply by content. If that were the case, then preachers could simply recite the Bible in their sermon and that would be enough.[2] To take it even a step further, if this were true, people could simply stay home, read their Bible and never come to church. But this is not the case and never has been the case. Why not? What does preaching accomplish that merely reciting the Bible cannot, or at least adds a necessary addendum that may not already be existing?

In order to better understand these reasons, we need only be reminded of our origins once more. This world and all of creation was created in perfection through God. This creation occurred through the speaking of the Word. Satan's speaking of a different word and Adam's believing in that word led to a fall in creation, leaving the world corrupted until the return of Christ. The coming of Christ into this world not only brought a new, redemptive Word into this world, but also came into this world as that very

---

1   John 20:31.

2   This could be considered a very "Gideon" approach to sharing the Word but in preaching rather than Bibles.

Word in the flesh Himself. Ever since the preaching of the *proto evangelium* in the Garden of Eden and then the fulfillment of that in Christ's flesh in the incarnation, there has been a new Word that has come into this world for all the world to see and hear through the person, work and message of Jesus Christ, which is still preached throughout this world.

The very nature and purpose of the Word of Jesus being preached is so that people might believe (in Christ) and by believing have eternal life. It is this Word that is being intentionally spoken through the preached Word and even in everyday Christian speech. What is unique about this speech is not so much that Christ is the manner of content. Rather, it is the spoken Christ who moves people from unbelief to belief, from death to life, from unholy to holy. It is this type of speaking that is true Christian preaching. It is this type of spoken Word that moves people from unbelief to belief. These terms are often spoken of by the Lutheran Church as the terms of "Law" and "Gospel." But it is vital that the Christian preacher not mistake himself into thinking he can simply speak these terms. What is vital in affording persons the opportunity to believe the Gospel is to have a movement from the state of Law to a state of Gospel.

It may have made a type of literary sense to first describe the terms Law and Gospel prior to speaking the usage of those terms. It would be similar to describing what a toddler's blocks are prior to first taking those blocks and stacking them in a certain way. However, it is important to understand the proverbial "blocks" so they may be used rightly. A sermon's ultimate goal is movement from Law to Gospel. Just as Christians are ones who have moved from death to life, so also do preachers move listeners from the death of the Law to the life that is in the Gospel.

The Law should not be seen or described as a "thing." It is better understood as an action.[3] The Law can most easily be described as that which shows us our sin. But even more so, the Law is a pronouncement from God Himself to all of creation, that due to the fall into sin, all people, animals, land and everything within nature has been corrupted. This is why creation is now called "fallen." Part and parcel of creation's fallen nature was not just death and disintegration of the physical but rather, as with the original fall of Satan, the greatest corruption happened when man turned away from

---

3   Throughout Romans 3 Paul speaks of the Law doing something to persons such as stopping every mouth (verse 19), being held accountable to God (verse 19), and falling short of the glory of God (verse 23) all of which are actions and not things.

believing in God as the sole provider and instead turned inward, to the self, for spiritual satisfaction. Because the heart, mind and soul have been corrupted, man does not have the power to turn toward God in faith and belief. Man was created by being face-to-face with God as He breathed the Gospel of life into the face of Adam.[4] But since the fall, man turned away and does not, in and of himself, have the power or ability to turn back to God on his own. This is the greatest effect of the fall into sin.

Now mankind no longer knows what we are missing. Since we lost a natural understanding and knowledge of God's goodness, we have no idea how evil Satan and his temptations are. This is why God provided the Law. The Law was given to show people their fallen state and was written by God to show man what creation should have continued to look like if not for the fall. The best evidence of this are God's Ten Commandments.

But what are the Ten Commandments for? Many denominations would say they were written so that people could keep them. The commandment says, "Do not kill," and a person does not kill. It makes sense to believe he has kept the commandment. If the commandment says, "Do not commit adultery" and a person does not commit adultery, then it would appear that the person has kept the commandment. And then that person, through his or her apparent ability to keep the Law, takes pride in himself and his spiritual pursuits, believing they are "right" in God's eyes. We need the Law. And we give thanks that the Law is holy and that the Commandments are holy and righteous and good.

Contemplating the Law without considering our fallen selves would be foolish to do. The Law is right and good. There is nothing wrong with the Law.[5] This is why God did not rewrite the Law after we fell into sin. The challenge is that we are now completely incapable of keeping the Law.[6]

To our sinful minds, this does not make sense. And by our own sinful natures, we do not understand these things of God. However, if we add to

---

4   "Then the Lord God formed the man of dust from the ground and breathed into his nostrils the breath of life, and the man became a living creature" (Genesis 2:7 [ESV]).

5   Romans 7:12–14 says, "So the law is holy, and the commandment is holy and righteous and good. Did that which is good, then, bring death to me? By no means! It was sin, producing death in me through what is good, in order that sin might be shown to be sin, and through the commandment might become sinful beyond measure. For we know that the law is spiritual, but I am of the flesh, sold under sin" (ESV).

6   Romans 3:19 says, "Now we know that whatever the law says, it says to those who are under the law, so that every mouth may be silenced and the whole world held accountable to God" (ESV).

this discussion an attempt to understand the Law according to some of St. Paul's words, we may understand more easily. St. Paul says, "The natural mind does not know the things of God" (I Cor. 2:14) and "The law was given so that we might become conscious of sin" (Rom. 3:20). These words of Paul here and throughout Romans help the Christian Church fully understand the true purpose of the Law. It was given so that sin might increase, and in that increase and by means of the increase, sinful man might fully understand his utter failure to appease God. In this respect, the Law succeeds in accomplishing what makes no sense to our rational, natural selves: we realize we are indeed sinners.

The Law was given mercifully by God so that the children of Adam might realize what is true about ourselves since the fall: from our births and by nature, we do not believe in God, turn our face to God, trust in Him, love Him, please Him and, in and of ourselves, could never do so. But God's desire is not just to have mankind understand that they are sinners. A physician may need to have a patient understand the greatness of his or her illness, only in so far as the ultimate desire of the physician is for the patient to understand that which will heal and make him or her live once again, specifically in a new and healed way that the patient never could have achieved on his or her own before. This is why God speaks not only His Law but ultimately desires to speak His Gospel to people. The Gospel might be most easily understood from Paul's words in Romans 3 where Paul says that a righteousness has been manifested apart from the Law (Rom. 3:21). It is one thing to be declared guilty by the Law that stands before our eyes, but it is something altogether different and wonderful to have the one who is guilty declared to be innocent. That is what the Gospel does.

The Gospel calls people to turn away from their sins. It invites people to stop listening to their accusatory consciences. The Gospel should never be confused with mere knowledge about Jesus. Many denominations will simply talk about Jesus or share facts about Him, speak about the culture of His life or anticipate what He ate and drank. But such talk misses the entire point of who Jesus is and why He came. Such talk is also relatively safe because it is dangerously neutral. It leaves people in the Law and simply presents a safe Jesus who is not calling people to a new life in Him. That is why preaching should never simply speak of Law and Gospel as static objects. They are not separate, non-existent things, nor are they two sides of the same coin.[7] Preaching the movement from Law to Gospel is God's ultimate action of bringing people from death and into life. If preaching fails to capture this repentant movement from death to life, it will inherently keep Jesus separate from His death (reason being the Law) and His resurrection (victory over the Law) and not allow the people to truly hear Good News.

The Good News for people is that in spite of their natural sin, in spite of their daily sin, in spite of the sins of the mind, God has declared them to be new people in Jesus. When people enter the waters of Baptism, they go in alone. But when they are brought out, they are connected with Christ and are found in Christ (Romans 6). Baptism was the first step, and then preaching takes hold when that new person comes out of the water. God calls Christians by name through preaching to turn and come back to Him, the One who welcomes them not with a stick to beat but with arms opened wide to embrace.

Man does not suffer in this life for the sake of his sins. Man suffers to be reminded that we are saved by grace and not by our own hands. There is no need for sinful man to suffer or for God to even punish man in this life. God punished His Son for our sin, and there is no payment man can make for sin that would make up for it. Man of himself cannot satisfy God or pay for his sin. That is why God does not punish people for sin in this life. If we could atone for our sins, then that would mean Jesus did not fully suffer for our sakes. And this is why the Gospel, in all its unabashed fullness, calls people to no longer consider their sin or mourn it, to no longer beat themselves up over their sin or remain in a sinful life. In Christ, mankind has been called and set free.

Little has been discussed about the movement from Law to Gospel in homiletical literature. Usually these terms are discussed separately as theological constructs. But perhaps the better and more precise way to discuss these terms is not to see them as static elements that somehow exist in and of themselves. Instead, these terms should be seen in a unified manner, tied together by the fall into sin and the grace that God promised and fulfilled in Christ. Preaching the Gospel is not a one-sided matter. The Gospel must be preached because sin has already happened. Going back to the creation, it is easy to see how God spoke a new Word to counter Satan's word. This new Word was one of hope and good news that Christ would come and be

---

7 Preachers should never view Law and Gospel as a form of "Yin/Yang" or other form of philosophical dualism.

punished for the sins of the whole world on the cross. It was in this speaking of the first Gospel that Adam and Eve were allowed to believe. They were invited to believe by that first redemptive sermon that God was going to bring about forgiveness for sin. It was this proclaimed Word that allowed Adam and Eve to believe in what Christ would do. And in believing once again, Adam and Eve were brought back to trusting in God, just as they had in the very beginning when God first created them.

IN-CLASS ACTIVITIES / GROUP DISCUSSION

1. Why was there an emphasis in discussing the movement from Law to Gospel? (Hint: Remember the children's blocks.)

2. What is the Law? What does it do?

3. Why is it important for us to know and be reminded we are sinners?

4. Read Rom. 3:20. Why was the Law given to us?

5. Why would God want us to see our increase in sin?

6. What does the Gospel do?

7. Read Rom. 3:20 again. How does that Gospel come to people?

OUT-OF-CLASS DISCUSSIONS / ASSIGNMENTS

1. What are some ways that most other Christians view Law and Gospel differently from Lutherans?

2. Why is it that God would not punish us for our sins in this life?

3. If Jesus was the one who was punished for all of our sins, then why do we still face suffering, temptation and sin in this world?

CHAPTER 8

Preaching the Bible

"The Word was made flesh."

—John 1:14

When a preacher preaches, the Bible is often heard. But sometimes it is not. Throughout the history of Christianity, the Scriptures have been viewed differently in regard to their role in preaching. There was a homiletical period in the Early Church in which Scripture was used as a proof-text and as substantiation for moral lessons. There were also periods throughout history in which the central role of Scripture was perhaps not emphasized.[1] Luther spoke of Germany being filled with preaching that centered upon fables and folk stories rather than the Scriptures.[2] In Europe and the United States, preaching was often affected by higher criticism.

Higher criticism greatly affected how people viewed the Scriptures. People began asking questions about the historical veracity of Scripture, its role in history and even questioning the personhood and divinity of Christ. Historical criticism was supposedly an attempt to engage the church in the textual and historical life of the Scriptures. However, the end result was that man once again attempted to place himself over and above the Word of God. The church was certainly effected in the fields of exegesis, history and

---

1   For a broad discussion of this topic see Paul Scott Wilson's *A History of Preaching*.

2   "The reason why the world is so utterly perverted and in error is that for a long time there have been no genuine preachers. There are perhaps three thousand priests, among whom one cannot find four good ones . . . and when you do get a good preacher, he runs through the gospel superficially and then follows it up with a fable about the old ass or a story about Dietrich of Berne, or he mixes in something of the pagan teachers, Aristotle, Plato, Socrates, and others, who are all quite contrary to the gospel, and also contrary to God, for they did not have the knowledge of the light which we possess." (Martin Luther, *Sermons I* [Philadelphia: Fortress Press, 1959], 51:64).

systematics. The effect on preaching was disastrous, and Europe and the United States are still suffering from its fallout.

In 1971 with the publication of *As One Without Authority*, a move was made to approach preaching differently. The reason was simple. There was a general belief among homileticians that the Scriptures were not inerrant, as was previously assumed, and were rather culturally bound. This meant that the Bible lacked authority, and if that were the case, then the pastors who preached those Scriptures did as well. Due to this generally prevailing sentiment, the preachers were encouraged to find another way to have people believe in Jesus without relying on the Scriptures as the primary place to know and believe in Jesus. The result is that preachers began to dabble in the usage of various rhetorical means to reach people especially through the use of narrative or storytelling. There was a commonly held belief that a narrative would be seemingly neutral and more readily received by hearers than recounting a Bible story or by listening to a pastor make any supposed truth statements. Regardless of the particular rhetorical discipline, the effect was the same: since Scripture was supposedly unable to carry Christ to people, preaching therefore needed to supposedly employ different tactics in order for people to believe in Jesus.

The Church has often wrestled with the question of Scripture's role in preaching. This confusion over God's Word began in Eden and will continue until Christ's return. But the Church does not have to abandon Scripture in her preaching. Preaching can be far more than merely stating an historical fact or proposing a nugget of wisdom for hearers to consider.

Every preacher ought to begin a sermon with Scripture. This is also the place where the preacher ends the sermon. This is not to say that churches and Christians will not continue to struggle with Scripture; it is in our nature to wrestle with God's Word. But thankfully for us and regardless of our misunderstandings and misreading of Scripture, Christ has promised that His Word will stand forever and be a testament for all generations.

The Word God brings can best be described homiletically—as was proposed earlier—as a Trinitarian preaching. When approaching the Scriptures, preachers should view them first and foremost as the means by which God is reaching out to His people. Through the Scriptures, something far greater happens than merely learning information or instilling morals. The Scriptures are more than merely teaching a historical lesson or separating

Law and Gospel. Ultimately, God, using His Scriptures, desires people to believe that salvation through Christ is theirs.

When preachers read the Scriptures, especially when they are the historical readings in the lectionary, they should always do so knowing that God desires to confront us in our sinfulness, recognize the state of our separation and then call us to believe that Christ has fulfilled the Law for us perfectly and that salvation is truly ours. For preachers, it is vital not only to read the Scriptures fully with this perspective, but also to read the particular biblical text, looking to see the salvation that God desires to bring through that text. God always desires the salvation of this creation and the people within it. God desires to save people from their sin. This is why the Scriptures are referred to as "Good News."

Good news is meant to be shared. It is not meant to be kept alone and isolated from others. It is meant to be shouted from the rooftops. Good news is something you run home and call a friend about. Sharing this good news might even have you speaking with complete strangers in marketplaces. The reason God's Good News is spread and shared is because God wants that Good News to be "for you." He wants every person to hear and believe that God's salvation is for them. This emphasis upon the individual is far different than the rampant individualism in which a single person can exist in isolation from the world and community. On the contrary, God wants individuals to hear His Good News. And as He does, He then longs to gather them around water, altar and confession, taking comfort that the Scriptures, God's promises, are truly for them.

In-Class Activity / Group Discussion

1. Throughout history, what are some ways that the Church has treated the Scriptures differently?

2. What was the challenge the Church faced with higher criticism and, in particular, following the publication of *As One Without Authority*?

3. The challenge with whether or not people believed Scripture was authoritative stretches back to Eden. When did this challenge first begin?

Out-of-Class Activities / Assignments

1. Preaching and the Scriptures are meant for far more than just merely imparting information, sharing history or telling morals. What are the Scriptures supposed to do in preaching?

2. If the Bible is truly for hearers to believe Christ is "for you," then it would be good to practice this homiletically. Select three biblical texts (Old Testament, Gospel, Epistle or Psalm), and explore different ways you could speak of these Scripture passages to people so they could believe they are "for you."

CHAPTER 9

Preaching Is "For You"

"The promise is for you and for your children."

—Acts 2:39 (ESV)

As long as creation continues, the Church will wrestle with the Scriptures. As the spoken, inerrant Word of God, the Bible will always be the battleground upon which the Church lives, dies and is martyred. God dwells bodily in His children through Jesus, and as such, the devil cannot stand for God's Word to dwell in them on account of Christ either. Rather, just like Adam and Eve, the devil desires to corrupt God's Word, and He especially does so through preaching. The Scriptures can be printed and remain relatively "unchanged" to a certain extent. But God's Word does not desire to remain frozen and stagnant. It is an unchanging Word that is willing to be clothed in the culture and contexts in which we find our lives, so that rich and poor, married or single, old or young—indeed, all sinners—might find comfort and faith in Jesus through these Words. But it is through these Words, the Words of preaching, that the devil chooses to attack most often.

Preaching can become corrupted in a variety of ways on different Sundays through the tens of thousands of preachers who preach and the hundreds of thousands of Christians who share God's Word on a daily basis with their friends and neighbors. This is the corruption of God's Word that has been forewarned to us in the Second Commandment: "You shall not misuse the name of the Lord your God. What does this mean? We should fear and love God so that we do not curse swear, use satanic arts, lie or deceive by His name but call upon it in every trouble, pray, praise and give thanks."[1] There are a myriad of ways that God's Word can be corrupted in preaching, but some are greater than others. This primer will highlight a few for preachers

---

1   Small Catechism, p. 11.

that, when properly understood and addressed, may help cover a multitude of sins.

During the fall, the devil twisted God's Word to Adam and Eve. He changed the prohibition against sin and the punishment for sin. But he also did something far more insidious: Satan had Eve and Adam believe that the Word of God was not for them, that it did not apply to them, that God's warning against eating would not happen and was not for their ears to hear. More than anything, Satan had Adam and Eve believe that God's Word was not written for "you."

The Law and Gospel are not written so that they can be spoken to the wind. The Scriptures were meant to be read to people. It was intended that people would hear these Words and believe that they were for them to hear and receive. Genesis does not record how Eve received the Words that God spoke, nor does it recount how Eve learned the prohibition against eating fruit from the tree. It is possible God spoke them directly to her since He did indeed walk among them in the garden. However, God did speak the Words directly to Adam. This is what leads many to believe that it was Adam who shared the words to Eve. This is one of the reasons why many churches do not ordain women, not because Eve was the first to sin. In God's ordering of creation, He was pleased to have His Word given to the husband, who would then be the one to disperse that Word among his wife and future children. Essentially, Adam "preached" to Eve about the prohibition, and Eve received that Word and believed it. But what so often happens to us happened to Eve: the devil snatched that Word away from her. He did it by having her believe that this Word was not spoken to her, that this Word did not belong to her.

As soon as a Christian does not believe the Word is for him, as soon as he believes the Word is for someone else (holier, different or otherwise), as soon as he forfeits Christ's work as his own, as soon as he thinks the Word isn't his, then the devil has won. When people cease believing the Word is for "you," they have already forfeited the claim that Christ has made upon them. They no longer believe that Christ, with all His work and deeds, belongs to them.[2]

And that is precisely what Satan did to Eve. He tempted her to forfeit the claim God's Word had upon her life and to cease believing. Instead of believing in God, she began to believe in herself. The creature ceased worshipping

---

2   Romans 6.

the Creator. The great corruption of nature Paul speaks about in Romans 3 all began with Eve when she ceased believing in God and began believing in herself. All this happened because she was deceived into believing that God's Word was not for her, that it no longer applied to her.

This is the great challenge for all preachers, whether we are preaching the Law or preaching the Gospel. If the people who are hearing cannot say this is about them, if they cannot pass that Word on to someone else, if they fail to see that Gospel is something that is given to them, then the preacher has failed in his holy task. The preacher will have succeeded in perpetuating the greatest of trespasses: the people will have been left comfortable in their sins, never hearing a Law that was about them, never having the chance to hear a Gospel that was for them.

But the greatest challenge of preaching is also the greatest joy. The Scriptures themselves provide preachers an unending show of convicting Law and resonating Gospel from which they can not only draw material for their sermons, but that can shape their very style of communication when it comes to the act of speaking Law and Gospel. John's Gospel provides us one of the very best illustrations of this fact. In it, he speaks as the voice of a narrator. It is written in a narrative style. It is as if we are watching a play of Jesus' life with all the characters living and breathing and moving accordingly throughout the story. Running parallel with these ever-changing scenes is the voice of the apostle John who is telling us everything that is going on. He is a true narrator, keeping his own focus and gaze upon the story, never looking at the audience so that he and they may together share in the significance of Christ's life.

John follows this pattern throughout his Gospel with the exception of one moment when John breaks this convention of writing style. He is dutifully recounting the story of Thomas and how Thomas did not believe. John faithfully recounts the story and ends with the second appearance of Jesus in which He invites Thomas to place his hand into Jesus' side, encouraging him to not doubt but believe. Jesus then says, "Blessed are those who have not seen and yet have believed" (John 20:29). But then John breaks down the walls between the proverbial narrator and audience as if he is turning directly toward those people reading this book, or those hearing this book, looking us in the eyes and saying, "Now Jesus did many other signs in the presence of the disciples which are not written in this book; but these are written so that *you* may believe that Jesus is the Christ, the Son of God, and that by believing *you* may have life in His name" (John 20:30–31; emphasis added).

This is quite a move for John and relatively abnormal in the Gospel. Matthew and Mark's Gospel retain a recounting emphasis. The Gospel of Luke begins by addressing a man named Theophilus who most likely paid to have this account researched and written. But then Luke switches to a narrative style and does not break that proverbial wall between the listener and the story. It is only John who makes that dramatic turn, shifting away from the narrative ever so briefly to remind the hearers, just in case they had forgotten or were not paying attention, that these things were written so that they may believe and by believing have eternal life. This is a kind move on John's part, and it forms a good homiletical foundation for all preachers. Preachers must never forget to say outright that the Gospel is for "you," the hearer, or even craft the message so that hearers might naturally insert themselves into the story of the Gospel.

There are many ways that preachers can allow people to become part of the Gospel story. Just recounting some of Jesus' parables shows that there are times when listeners are automatically to see themselves in the story.[3] Preachers may not always speak in a parabolic fashion, but modern preachers can and should include the congregation in their sermon so they know they are a part of God's story and that salvation is for them. Perhaps this could occur in the recounting of a scriptural story, allowing people to see themselves as the different characters. The parable of the prodigal son is certainly one that would allow hearers to relate to many different people. Such a parable could find hearers recalling how they have been in that same situation as the brother, or sadly remembering the times they were the man who left, or even recalling the times when they were acting as the father.

Certainly preachers can find times when people might relate to parables in specific ways. However, preachers should be careful not to fall into the trap of passing a gimmick off as the preaching of Law and Gospel. It is an interesting exercise to discover how we might all relate to the characters of the prodigal son story, but we should never forget that ultimately our story is one of the relationship between our trinitarian God and us. When we place God as the primary actor within the story, we find ourselves situated a bit differently in these parables. Although the parables retain a quality of

---

3   A good example / rule of thumb would be those instances in which Jesus names the Pharisees specifically.

finding that relational element for us, all of a sudden people are looking into the eyes of God within this story, and they see themselves being the ones whose sin has become evident. In spite of that sin, the Father (God) is willing to sacrifice of Himself so that He might stoop down and receive back into His arms His wayward son (us) who has committed terrible, foul and utterly embarrassing actions. In spite of our sins and even in full view of them, God opens His arms and receives us fully as His pure, innocent and forgiven children. It is one thing for people to find that relational element within a parable or given story, but it is another thing altogether when God is inserted into the equation and we take our rightful places in relation to Him. When this occurs, we are invited to sit before our God and see His graciousness toward us. He is the one who breaks down the wall, inviting us to come forward to receive comfort in Him and Him alone.

The Law and Gospel are truly for "you." If the preacher speaks in such a way that the hearer does not know salvation is for "you" (i.e., "it is mine"), then the preacher might as well have never preached in the first place. When two people are playing catch with a ball, what good does it do for a thrower to throw 50 feet over someone's head? The desire is for a person to catch the ball, not watch it fly over his head. That is the nature of the Gospel. It is meant to be caught by people so they can believe it is "for you." This holds true for members of the congregation who are seven years old, 30 years old or 80 years old. Preachers must preach so all the people may catch the Word, receive it, believe it as being for them and, by believing, have their life in Christ strengthened and reconfirmed every week. It is not such a bad thing to happen in this dying world!

So far we have discussed a way to interpret Scripture. But interpreting Scripture and believing Scripture are not always synonymous. The best way for people to believe Scripture is for those people to believe that Scripture is written for them. Keep in mind what the apostle John says: "These are written so that you may believe that Jesus is the Christ, the Son of God, and that by believing you may have life in His name" (John 20:31). John's Gospel was not written so it could sit on a shelf or be used only as an historical document. It was written so that you, yes, YOU, might believe in Jesus and by believing already be a possessor of eternal life. The Bible is God's love letter to you. It was crafted and shaped by God with the purpose of waking you up to realize the cataclysmic tragedy that occurred in the fall, but then to place you in the arms of your loving Savior. Since the Scriptures were written for you, then likewise the preacher's sermon should by spoken for you.

In-Class Activity / Group Discussion

1. Read a parable, and identify how persons might openly "relate" or "identify" with the characters.

2. Read the same parable from a perspective in which God enters into it and works salvation for "you," the hearer.

3. Tell a more local story or parable of modern life in which people might identify. Keep the story less than 10 sentences.

4. Using the same story, tell how God might speak to people in terms of Law, Gospel or both.

5. What did the apostle John do differently in His Gospel?

6. What does John remind us is important in preaching?

Out-of-Class Activities / Assignments

1. Take an older sermon and note those instances when you have said that either the Law or the Gospel is "for you," a hearer, to believe.

2. Find those instances in an older sermon when this was not accomplished. Rewrite those passages in such a way that they are now intended to be "for you" to hear.

CHAPTER 10

PREPARING

"Prepare the way of the Lord."

—John the Baptist (Luke 3)

When asked how a preacher will prepare for a sermon, a person will hear many different remarks. Sometimes the style of delivery will affect a preacher's preparation. For example, if a preacher chooses to preach in an extemporaneous manner in which he will dwell upon a text, he might not write anything; or if he does write something, it may be a few words on a piece of paper with little formal preparation involved. In the case of extemporaneous preachers, it is good to note that while they may not write anything down, they certainly spend time thinking through their sermon and what it is they are going to preach about; whether they want to admit that or not is a different matter entirely.[1]

Other preachers will say they prepare for preaching differently. There are some preachers and preaching traditions that will say they do impromptu speaking with no preparation. They will often mark spontaneity as evidence of the Holy Spirit being present. However, digging into their practice shows they generally do think of a text and have even thought out a general theme and outline beforehand. There are some preachers who are trained well

---

1 Bruce Rosenberg made some excellent observations when it came to the supposed phenomena of impromptu/extemporaneous preaching within the African American Church. Whereas through most outsiders' eyes it would appear genuine (or Spirit-driven as many preachers would propose), in reality though Rosenberg showed how the preachers were often preoccupied throughout the week about their upcoming sermon even to the point of using language, terminology, and sermon patterns in normal everyday communication as a proverbial "run up" to the preaching event that weekend. See Bruce Rosenberg, *Can These Bones Live? The Art of the American Folk Preacher* (Chicago: University of Chicago Press, 1988), 40.

enough (or fake it) so that a Bible can be opened and they could preach from any random passage. This could reflect proper oratorical training and is not difficult to do and do well when necessary. There are others, however, who incessantly babble over randomness. Keep in mind that just because a man is preaching from a pulpit does not mean that such speaking should always be considered preaching.

There are still yet other preachers who lean more toward a desired preparatory method but maybe don't have the skills to do so on their own. Numerous pastors will know the text the prior week since it comes from a lectionary, but they will purposely wait until Saturday evening to write their sermon. This is rarely a good practice for pastors to employ since it allows for no reflection upon the written sermon. This practice can also place an undue burden upon the pastor and his family.

And yet there are still other groups who will swing the pendulum in the opposite direction and spend so much time in sermon preparation that they will translate all three readings for the day into their original language. These preachers will then glean through every commentary about the texts, basically absorbing the thoughts and opinions of perhaps five authors or more, each of whom may have different thoughts and approaches to the text. Then the preacher will swoon over the mountain of notes he has taken, trying to wed the texts together into a single thought, piecing multiple texts together into some odd Frankenstein-like monster. This type of over-preparation most often results in sermons that have different themes from the various authors and do not match up well together in the final product of the sermon.

It can be very confusing to consider where to start the sermon writing process. The above are all very real examples and lived practices of many good and faithful preachers. More on these specifics will be shared later in this chapter. But before commentaries are cracked open and coffee is poured, before pastors get together to share ideas with one another and translate a text into its original language, perhaps there is something else to consider. Perhaps a preacher should stand back from the text a moment and realize what God wants to do through this preached Word.

Why do we preach? Or better yet, why does God have us preach? Does the preacher have some special ability that is allowing him to preach, or is the preacher the one who has simply been called to be the one in the congregation to open his mouth? If a preacher forgets who he is, or where he came from, he runs the risk of becoming arrogant like the devil, enamored with his own abilities and forgetful of the fact that the only ability given to that pastor stems from God, the only One able to give the forgiveness of sins. But even beyond a preacher becoming enamored with himself, the greater sin is when the preacher forgets what God does in His Word: that the promise of Christ is for God's people and that they can believe in the works of Christ as that which truly saves them from all sin, death and the power of the devil.

It may be best for all preachers to remember who they are before they make any sermon preparations. They should remember the fall and how it has affected them. These suggestions could be taken as a means by which the preacher might keep his ego in check, which is certainly always good. However, there is something far greater at stake. If the preacher fails to realize that God is a God who creates and re-creates through His Word, then that preacher's preaching will never be satisfactory. If the preacher fails to realize that Satan was the first murderer and his weapon of choice was twisting God's Word so Adam and Eve would follow him rather than God, then that preacher will experience challenges in his preaching. If that preacher fails to understand that through the speaking of the Word, God makes promises to us and that through Christ we can trust and believe those promises not merely as intellectual fact but as matters of faith, then he will never preach the type of spoken Word that God has demanded His preachers to speak. If the preacher fails to believe that through preaching not only does God speak, but that this speaking bestows the very thing of which it speaks—forgiveness of sins—then he could actually end up preaching falsely.[2]

But if a pastor does realize what God does through preaching, then his sermons will be different. They may not be the greatest oratorical events in history, nor should they strive for that (although it is not bad to have both!). What is vital though is that the sermon offers hearers the chance to hear and believe in Jesus Christ and to have their faith in Him strengthened. To accomplish this does not require great rhetorical flair or the skill of a poet or the voice of a great theatrical actor. What it does require is a pastor in faith who speaks of Christ's mercy to us through His suffering, death and resurrection and reminds his parishioners that all of Christ's work belongs to the hearer. To such a preacher, the angels themselves will fall on their knees as

---

2   "Through this office of preaching and of forgiving sins, souls are resurrected here from sins and from death" (Luther, *Word and Sacrament II*, 299.)

they weep in joy for hearing the wondrous mercies of the One whom they adore day in and day out for all eternity. To such a faithful pastor, they will truly hear Jesus say, "Well done, My good and faithful servant."

Preachers should base their sermons off the Bible. This may seem to be a no-brainer for some, and for others this may seem offensive to even state, but it needs to be said clearly. Over the past 50 years in particular, there has been a general move away from the Scriptures as that which is seen as authoritative, normative and transformative in the lives of believers and unbelievers alike. Few today would say that it is simply the Word of God alone that converts. They would typically add something to that sentiment. In addition, higher criticism has left the Western Church with a dissected view of the Scriptures. In many churches, the sermon has become a hollowed out version of God's Word. In some instances, entire denominations now view the Scriptures as they would someone who has been emasculated: there is no power left.

But such a view is simply untrue for many Lutherans.[3] Lutherans can and should always believe that the Scriptures are the means by which God speaks an inerrant, eternal Word to His people. It is from this Word that the Church knows anything at all about God and thus debunks those charismatics who would claim that they are the wellspring to know God rather than the Scriptures which have been testified to by all the prophets, apostles and martyrs. The Scriptures are the means by which God Himself has selected to come to His people throughout the ages. They are the way God has decided to write and speak to those who have never seen Him or met Him during Christ's earthly ministry so that they also may have the opportunity to know and believe in Jesus. This is why preachers preach on the Scriptures.

How this occurs is a curious thing. A preacher does not simply stand in the pulpit and read a page from the Bible. Nor do preachers currently stand and read the entire letter of Paul to the Church in Rome or in Corinth.[4] It is commonly expected that when the preacher stands in the pulpit he will fulfill two functions: (1) He will preach from a biblical text and (2) He will bring a "new" Word of God to the congregation. In this sense, "new" should

---

3   Please note I am writing this with The Lutheran Church—Missouri Synod generally in mind and am in no way referring to the Evangelical Lutheran Church of America who has done everything in its power to neuter God's Word.

4   Although this was done in the Early Church and indeed was the reason why the epistles were written in the first place.

not be taken as an addendum to the Scriptures nor to be as authoritative in the same sense as the Scriptures. And yet, Luther proposed that very thing, saying that the preached Word from God is to be as reliable as the Scriptures and held up in the same light as an equal manifestation of the proclamation of Christ.[5]

At first glance, it may seem odd, contradictory or even impossible to make the assertion Luther does. How can a preacher preach a Word that is not meant to be written down as if it were a new part of the canon of existing biblical texts, and yet, at the same time, say that such a Word is equal or even superior to that of the biblical texts?

But preachers can do this. This feat is accomplished whenever a preacher speaks Christ in such a way that hearers may believe that His death and resurrection has now been given to them. The sinless One has been given to sinners so that they are now sinless too. The One who was truly free came to those who are bound so that they are now made free in Him. The One who was clean has been given to the guilty so that the guilty can now say that they themselves are clean.

Our attention now turns to exactly what it is a preacher preaches. The preacher does not stand in a pulpit and merely read Scripture, although this may occur. The preacher also does not have complete freedom to say whatever he wants or to tell whatever story or joke he wants. By virtue of entering the pulpit, the preacher willingly chains himself to the proclamation of the Gospel in Christ as a manner of content (as to what is said) and as a matter of function (meaning how it is said and the intent of how Words are spoken). And by doing so, he makes a confession that what is important in preaching is not simply what is said, but the goal behind what is said: that hearers are to be given the opportunity to believe that what Jesus Christ accomplished in this world was done for them.

Ideally, each person should be able to say after every single sermon that he or she heard Jesus Himself speak to and deliver him or her in some way from this world and from sin, death and the power of the devil by means of Jesus' own life, death and resurrection given to him or her. This does not mean that every single sermon will take up every single theme the same time every single Sunday. Preaching should be considered as a full and

---

5   Richard Lischer, *Theories of Preaching* (Durham: Labyrinth Press, 1987), 95; Donald McKim, *The Bible in Theology and Preaching* (Nashville: Abingdon Press, 1985), 197; David Buttrick, *A Captive Voice: The Liberation of Preaching* (Louisville: Westminster John Knox Press, 1994), 26.

healthy diet that a person consumes over a lifetime; a person doesn't eat all food at once. One day he or she may eat meat, the next day rice, the other day vegetables. These meals will change and adapt over the years and yet still be a healthy food that sustains a person. Likewise, preaching should not attempt to cover the whole counsel of God or all matters of Christian faith in one sermon, and yet each sermon should be a healthy serving of the Gospel by which people will have the chance to once again be filled with the goodness of Christ, whose life, death and resurrection occurred so that they could be set free from death, guilt and shame.

In-Class Activity / Group Discussion

1. What is the proper understanding of where the sermon truly originates?

2. It is true the Holy Spirit causes faith in the hearts of men. It is also true the Holy Spirit works through means such as the Scriptures to cause people to believe in Jesus. Knowing this to be true, how should the preacher approach the Scriptures when preparing to preach?

3. Why is it important for a preacher to remember who he is before beginning his sermon preparation?

Out-of-Class Activities / Assignments

1. There are many different ways to write a sermon. Some preachers write out full manuscripts, others use an outline and still others may write a few points on a paper. Try a method in class that you would not normally use. What were the benefits and challenges with each?

2. What are the two "functions" a preacher fulfills when he steps into the pulpit? In what way should these tasks be approached in light of Luther's comments?

CHAPTER 11

Sermon Preparation Worksheet, Part 1

> "Satan, hear this proclamation; I am baptized into Christ!"
>
> —*Lutheran Service Book*, #594, st. 3

Preachers are to consider the Bible a certain way. The previous chapter established that preaching from the Scriptures does not mean merely repeating them. Rather, the Scriptures allow preachers to preach the eternal Word once more, spoken in such a way that would allow hearers to believe that what Christ has done has been done for them.

Selecting a Scripture passage to preach on can be relatively easy to do. Preachers should generally follow a Church Year lectionary that will provide the readings for each Sunday of the year. These various Scripture passages will supply the preacher and his congregation with a well-rounded diet of God's Word. There may be other occasions such as funerals or weddings in which a scriptural text would need to be selected to fit the occasion. Such texts should be chosen with concern for the particular event and in faithfulness to the Word Christ should proclaim at these events (i.e., hope at the death of a faithful Christian).

Once an appropriate text has been selected, the preacher can begin the sermon-writing process. In order to write the sermon (eventually), it is vitally important for the preacher to engage in a bit of preparatory work. This work is important for every preacher regardless of whether he chooses to preach from a Post-It note or from a full-blown manuscript. The intent is to allow the preacher the chance to select a single theme from a passage for the benefit of the hearers. Although identifying the topic or theme is not discussed often in the homiletical community,[1] it is a vital practice for preachers to adopt.

The greatest challenge modern preachers face is their inability to select a SINGLE theme for a sermon. Unfortunately, this may become an ever increasing challenge for those societies who fail to teach some form of grammar or composition even at the elementary level of education. If for some reason a preacher decides to have five themes covered in a 15- or 20- minute sermon, then there is no doubt the hearer will be unable to listen or understand. It doesn't matter how good the content is; it will be drowned out by a multiplicity of themes all pressing for time and attention. When preachers preach multi-themed sermons, the end result is a simple one and a deathblow for any preacher: people will stop listening. The greatest challenge for modern preachers lies not just from the preaching of a false or dead God (which indeed is rampant) but in perpetuating a type of preaching in which hearers (including the children and elderly) have to work very hard to find a central point or thought.

The people of God do want to hear a good Word from the Lord on Sunday. They yearn to hear a Word from God in the sermon and are very hopeful to hear the Gospel every single Sunday. As such, forcing a congregation to dig through a mountain of semi-fleshed ideas is probably not the best way to encourage people to listen to the sermon. How sad for the people of God when preachers force them to dig through a mountain of material! Jesus is the One who comes searching for us; we have not been called to go searching for Him. The people of God often need a water fountain, not a firehose.

Preachers should not necessarily view themselves as different from the rest of the congregation when it comes to the sermon-writing process. It is simply that the preacher is the one who has been called by God to be the first to enter the world of the Scriptures for the sake of bringing a Word back out from the Scriptures and to the people. The preacher goes to the Scriptures on behalf of the congregation to be the first one to hear the Word of the Lord, be affected by that Word through Law and Gospel, and then come out of those Scriptures filled with the goodness and mercy of God through Christ.[2]

It is always a challenge to know what to look for when reading a text in preparation to preach on the text. It is very easy for a preacher to become

---

1   A notable exception is Paul Scott Wilson's *The Four Pages of the Sermon*.

2   Thomas Long, *The Witness of Preaching* (Westminster John Knox Press, 1989), 3.

lost in the cultural nuances of a text and spend more time reading about wash basins rather than reading of the One who is doing the washing. By overly concentrating upon incidentals, a preacher could unwittingly so isolate Jesus within a piece of history that He becomes essentially located only within that time and space rather than becoming the One who rules over all time and space. Preachers should never forget that when dealing with the Scriptures, they are not dealing with a mere record of culture or history. Although it may do these things, that is not Scripture's main purpose. Jesus, the Word Himself, spoke about this when He said to the Pharisees, "You search the Scriptures because you think that in them you have eternal life; and it is they that bear witness about Me" (John 5:39).

When preachers begin their preaching task, they should always remember to whom they are going. The Scriptures are not just a book or a record of history. They do not just talk about Jesus. Through the Scriptures and in the preached Word, the Creator of the universe has been pleased to dwell. Through, in and under these Words, God Himself chooses to bring salvation to all of creation. Whether these are the Words and promises He attaches to water in Baptism or the Words guaranteeing His presence to people in the Lord's Supper, this is how Jesus chooses to act. Through the Word of preaching, people are invited to leave their sins behind and find fullness, freedom and forgiveness in Him, Words that should shape the form of any sermon.

Getting to this point of proclaiming the Gospel will take time and patience for preachers. Preachers are just like everyone else; they are creatures of the fall. Preachers, however, are being asked to do something that is contrary to their nature and contrary to the nature of all people. They are asked to speak a completely free and unhindered Gospel to people. Such a speaking is foreign to us. Why some preachers can suppose they could just do such an alien task without preparation, theological reflection or practice is mesmerizing to consider.

A very common misperception within the Church is that preachers will naturally become better over time.[3] But such a way of thinking about preaching can actually prevent the Church from improving her spoken Word. The

---

3 Many mistakenly believe that older preachers are better than younger preachers because of their experience. Although we would like to think that people perfect over time like a fine wine, that is not always the case. Sometimes bad habits, uncorrected, become reinforced over time and solidified in practice. Also, never forget it is the Word of God that brings salvation, not a man's age.

Church would never be inclined to say that a sinner will just become less sinful over time (although some heterodox churches may say that), so why would the faithful think this about preaching? If the sinner does not lessen his sin over time (on an intrinsic level), then why should it be supposed the sinful preacher would somehow improve over time? In addition, preachers face their own personal distractions that can pull their focus away from concentrating on a sermon and its preparations. Care for wives and children, the needs of congregations and calls and the work preachers do to support themselves and their congregational life can all distract preachers from sermon preparation, making it seem more like a work than a blessing.

Many preachers admit that they despise preparing a sermon and try to put it off until the last minute. In these cases, preachers often lack a decent method to assist them in their sermon writing. Sermon preparation should not be work for the preacher. Sermon preparation and preaching should relax, encourage and strengthen a preacher as he, along with the congregation, basks in the goodness and mercy of God, who loves us enough to come in our flesh and rescue us from our sins. The task of sermon preparation includes the joy of discovering God's goodness toward us in Christ and something that can be joyous for preachers. If the preacher possesses the appropriate tools to assist him in his preparation, then he and the whole congregation benefit greatly.

Below is a proposed "Sermon Preparation Worksheet" that preachers can use when they are first observing a text for preaching. This is a worksheet that helps guide a preacher's exploration of a scriptural text and asks certain questions. It can also be a tool to focus the preacher's attention by looking at the text with God's desire to bring salvation into this world through preaching. After the preacher completes his "Sermon Preparation Worksheet," he will be encouraged to focus these thoughts more fully by shaping them into the "Pages Worksheet." The latter will become the crux of the sermon. Once the "Pages Worksheet" has been completed, the preacher should feel confident in writing his sermon. When following these guidelines, the preacher will explore a scriptural text in such a way as to hopefully allow the Gospel to have predominance and to have optimal impact for the congregation.

Below is a description of the components that will make up a "Sermon Preparation Worksheet." These are written to assist the preacher from the beginning of his sermon preparation (i.e., reading the text) all the way through to the actual writing of the sermon. This worksheet can become an excellent resource to assist the preacher in exploring the text in a way that allows God to remain the living actor in the lives of people, while assisting the preacher in contemplating how to keep salvation free from the efforts of man.

SERMON PREPARATION WORKSHEET COMPONENTS

Identifying the Text. This task has been mentioned briefly in a previous chapter. Selecting a biblical text— and the right one—is critical when preaching. It is strongly recommended that all students and preachers follow a common lectionary. A lectionary will ensure that God's people are receiving a healthy diet of God's Word throughout the year. When preachers do not follow a lectionary, they tend to select texts on their own. When preachers become the ones to make such selections, their sermons often become stale over time due to their selection of similar, personal favorites. Their preaching also suffers when focusing upon God as the actor in the text for the simple reason that these texts are perceived as being "owned," to a certain degree, by the preacher and he may find it difficult to allow God to be the actor. In addition, since many personal favorites often come from the Epistles, these readings fail to find a residence within the Gospels, which often speak of Jesus very clearly as the main actor in God's narrative of salvation toward us. Preachers should preach primarily from the Gospel within a given lectionary for the Sunday Divine service. For the midweek service or any morning or evening gatherings, it is common to preach upon the Old Testament or Epistle readings assigned for that day. During special occasions such as funerals, weddings or dedications, the preacher should select texts appropriate to the given situation and ones that are recommended within various hymnal lectionaries for such events.

*When appropriate, take a moment and write the selected **biblical text** in your Sermon Preparation Worksheet.*

God Is the Actor. In preaching, God is ultimately the One who is doing an action. There are some texts in which this is overt and easy to see. Jesus may be mentioned by name as well as perhaps God the Father or the Holy Spirit. Sometimes God may not be mentioned by name, but it is still easy to see God being the actor since the actions are only ones God can accomplish (i.e., the forgiving of sins). There are a surprising number of texts that do not explicitly mention God by name and a surprising number of preachers do the same when they are preaching on these texts.[4] When there is a text in which God is not mentioned by name, it is critical to name who God is "behind the text." This means that the Scriptures should always be viewed as a record of God's actual actions and doings. For example, in the parable of the Good Samaritan, God is not mentioned by name.[5] And yet in the parable of the Good Samaritan and others, God is still the main actor. He is the major character and initiator of change in the narrative.

If the preacher fails to realize this, the sermon will almost automatically degenerate into a moral tale espousing hearers to do some work of the Law. In the case of this particular parable, that may be the preacher spurring on hearers to be "better neighbors to each other" or maybe encouraging people to "slow down and not move too fast" or to "take time and smell the roses" or some other such silly thing. The point is, however, if God is absent, then so is salvation. It is important for the preacher to not only see this for himself when doing his sermon preparation, but for him to also be able to name the God who is behind these texts so that the listeners may also see, know and believe.

*Once the text has been read several times, take note specifically how God is being named in this text and even more so, how God is acting in this text. take a moment and answer the appropriate exploring questions in your Sermon Preparation Worksheet. Feel free to also add other observations you may have noticed about **how God is acting** to the side of these questions. This worksheet is for your usage and your benefit in sermon preparation.*

Jesus Is Our Redeemer. Whether the Triune God is mentioned by name or not, all Scripture ultimately leads us to the cross. In reading a biblical text, it is always good to see where Jesus is in that text. Preachers should identify Jesus throughout all the Old Testament Scriptures as well. Even when Jesus is not directly referenced or foreshadowed in some way, the preacher should always remember that the Law was given to show people how powerless they are to do anything about sin, which ultimately leads them to Jesus, the only One who can free mankind from the effect of the Law (Rom. 3).

Identifying Jesus in a text and the salvation only Jesus can bring is

---

4 Paul Scott Wilson, *The Four Pages of the Sermon: A Guide to Biblical Preaching* (Nashville: Abingdon Press, 1999) 40.

5 In fact, God is often not mentioned by name in Jesus' parables and yet is always the main actor.

*critical in any sermon. There is no gospel without Jesus and God's goodness shown to us through Christ. During this section of the worksheet take time to explore the biblical text noting **how Jesus is redeeming us**. Note what Jesus is doing, and what He is saying. When there is a passage in which Jesus may seem absent in the Old Testament or an epistle, always link that reading back to the person and work of Christ in His death and resurrection for us. As Jesus said, the Scriptures "bear witness about Me" (John 5:39).*

The Holy Spirit Brings Belief. Preachers should always remember that the Scriptures and the sermon are meant to be gifts to real, living, breathing people. The Old Testament was not written to be a mere historical record. It was read out loud when the congregation gathered. The Epistles were not written to collect dust on a shelf. They were all written with the intent of being read publicly within a congregation. Likewise, the sermon is meant to be preached to real people so that a real God might come to these people who are hurting every day because of real sin, unbelief and death. If the sermon's main goal is to allow people the opportunity to believe in Christ and by believing have eternal life, then sermon preparation should take this into account.

The Holy Spirit points people back to the works of God in Jesus who brings us salvation and to the ways that God has worked salvation for us. Note those instances in which people are encouraged to **believe in the works of God that have been done "for you." The Holy Spirit may not always be specifically mentioned in a sermon because He is satisfied in pointing to Christ and testifying to the salvation He brings us.*

ACTIVITY: PRACTICING THE SERMON PREPARATION WORKSHEET

1. Students should select one of the following biblical texts (Ps. 23; Matt. 5; Matt. 10:34–39; Luke 8:22–25; Luke 15:1–7; John 11:17–27; John 20:24–29; Rom. 7:1–6; Gal. 3:10–14). If students have not already been assigned a specific biblical text for preaching, feel free to have them either select one of the above or assign it for them. The above biblical texts provide good examples to engage the exercises in this primer. Complete the "Sermon Preparation Worksheet" found in the Appendix. Students may also select a different text with their teacher's permission if they are scheduled to preach soon. Instructors may also

choose to assign texts and have preachers preach an actual sermon in class in front of their peers. It is sometimes more appropriate to begin preaching publicly with short paragraphs rather than full sermons. Instructors may also choose to work through each of the phases of (1) identifying God as the actor, (2) identifying Jesus as our redeemer, and (3) identifying our belief in God's works for us, by means of assigning the texts to students and having them write a longer paragraph. Students could then present their prepared paragraphs in class for #1 on the first day, #2 during the next class and so on. This allows for a multitude of examples to be seen as students engage the practice and also allows students the opportunity to preach shorter sections in from of the class If there are no scheduled preaching events on a student's calendar, then he should be encouraged to select a text of his choosing and preach it to an "imaginary" congregation, keeping his home congregation in mind).

*Note to instructors: It is always good to have students preach a sermon they have prepared in front of their peers. When doing so, please make sure they have followed the guidelines as discussed in this chapter. Students should not be permitted to preach a sermon they have already written; rather, they should write a new sermon based on the techniques already discussed. When preaching before their peers, have the students preach in a worshipping space or chapel whenever possible. Even though this is a class, the students are still handling the Word of God and speaking the Gospel, which should always be held in the highest esteem. If time allows, and the instructor is able, it is always good to have preaching students present their sections to the instructor for private review prior to sharing before the class. This allows the instructor the chance to change any gross errors and also allows the student to have confidence that their final preaching sectional will be of good quality. This also benefits the entire class. The class will now be hearing good examples from the entire group. It is often the practice of having preachers present their material for the first time in front of the class. This is not an optimal practice and only ensures that preaching sectionals of a poorer quality will be shared with the group rather than excellent ones—a much better practice for all.

CHAPTER 12

SERMON PREPARATION WORKSHEET, PART 2

"Death, you cannot end my gladness; I am baptized into Christ!"

—*Lutheran Service Book*, #594, st. 4

In the previous chapter, students had the opportunity to select a biblical text, identify the actor (God) in it, note how salvation occurs and indicate how that salvation impacts "you," the hearer. These are critical pieces in sermon preparation and play a vital role in writing a sermon that centers on God's work of salvation in this world. Without identifying these elements within a text, a sermon could be written in which God is not a central figure or is merely mentioned as a passive entity. Salvation has also been clearly identified as that which comes from God, and that must be identified within the text. This allows the preacher, in his subsequent sermon, to speak the Gospel clearly for his hearers. And finally, the work completed so far has also allowed the student to see that salvation is not only for them, but will also be for anyone who hears the sermon. The hearers will know that this Gospel is for "you."

The current chapter will take up a continued discussion of the students' "Sermon Preparation Worksheet" by concentrating on the creation of a theme for the sermon. Themes are very important for sermons. They act as a type of theological flagpole in that they state what it is we as Christians believe and confess. They also act as visible reminders to the preacher that if he starts to wander too far away, the theme can help maneuver his sermon back to the central message.

Writing a "Theme" Statement

Perhaps the most influential component of the "Sermon Preparation Worksheet" is the writing of a theme sentence. A theme is what ties together the actions of God in the text and propels the preacher toward the actual shaping of his sermon in such a way that salvation in Jesus Christ is always emphasized. The theme sentence should also be viewed as a tool the preacher uses throughout the sermon-writing process. It is not a tool that sits passively upon the preacher's workbench once it has been created. Instead, the theme sentence should be in the preacher's hand as he engages the biblical text and especially as he writes and edits his sermon.

Most preachers will admit that they do not like using tools to prepare their sermons, but preachers should realize that any tool feels foreign when first using it. A hammer may feel awkward in the hands of a novice. A chisel will probably slip out of the hands of someone who has never used this tool to create. Likewise for preachers, tools can seem foreign in the sermon-writing process. But once a preacher uses these tools, in particular the theme sentence, and learns how to master them, he may lament that he didn't do so sooner and would never consider abandoning such tools in the future.

In order to better understand what a theme sentence can accomplish for the preacher and how it can best be used as a helpful tool in sermon writing, it needs to be defined first. For the sake of sermon writing, the **theme** is defined as *a declarative sentence identifying God's redeeming actions used by the preacher to help shape the content of his sermon.*

Identifying a theme sentence can be a great challenge for any preacher. And believe it or not, this effort should take up a good majority of the preacher's time. Preachers may be surprised to hear that they should spend a large amount of time at the beginning of their sermon-writing process on the creation of a single sentence. Most preachers want to jump right in and begin writing their sermons. However, jumping in to the sermon-writing process without having first identified a clear and productive theme will force the preacher to spend countless hours rewriting his sermon because it just doesn't feel "right" (if the preacher notices this at all). If such need for a revision is not caught and a sermon is preached without possessing a strong central theme, people will be confused and stop listening. Instead, they will drift off into a daydream about their activities for the rest of the day, make up shopping lists in their head, think about challenges at work or just take those moments to grab a quick nap.

Although identifying a theme sentence can be challenging and can take up a disproportionate amount of time in writing one sentence when compared to the entirety of a sermon, there are ways to assist the preacher in this task. As the preacher becomes more accustomed to this practice, he will face fewer and fewer challenges in writing those themes. In a short amount of time, the preacher can see this practice as a positive one and one he has no desire to stop utilizing. In order to write a theme sentence from a biblical text that can be used in the sermon-writing process, there are three components to consider. Following these three guidelines should help the preacher create a theme that will be a helpful tool for him in writing his sermon every week:

a) **The theme should identify God's actions.** The theme sentence must answer the question: "What is God doing in this text?"[1] Sermons should ultimately be about God's actions in saving us and this world. Because of this, the theme sentence must clearly articulate what God is doing for salvation. For example, perhaps a preacher is preaching on the text of the raising of Lazarus. A good theme sentence emphasizing God's actions could be "God is still calling the dead to live again in Him" or "Jesus is calling people to believe and have eternal life in Him right now." Throughout this particular text, Jesus is very active. Note how the two examples above name God as the One who is doing the action either as "God" or more specifically as "Jesus."

Sometimes a text may be less clear about God's actions. For example, in the text that speaks of John the Baptist preparing the way for the Lord, Jesus Himself is not specifically mentioned.[2] When instances like this occur, the preacher should reread the text, noting the Law and the Gospel. Whenever a preacher has identified the Law and the Gospel in a text, he can then specifically name the One who is the only salvation from the Law that condemns us. For example, in the text above, an appropriate theme sentence could be "Jesus is always coming as the One who removes sin from the world even when we can't see Him" or "God sends people to speak His comfort to us." In both of these examples, God has become the actor within the text and the sermon, even though God is not listed as one of the acting agents within the biblical text.

---

1   Wilson, *Four Pages*, 39.

2   Matthew 3:1–12. Granted, the Holy Spirit is mentioned as "winnowing," but "Jesus" is not mentioned, which is somewhat unique in a Gospel passage.

Often it can be a challenge to identify the Law and the Gospel in order to find out exactly what God may be doing in the biblical text. When these instances occur, the preacher should ask several simple questions to help highlight Law and Gospel so that the preacher can see exactly what God is doing. The preacher could ask of the text, "When are people shown their sin within this text?" This sin may be manifested in several ways: the broken relationship between God and man or God's anger or displeasure over the failings of man. There may also be other times when the effects of the fall into sin are prevalent: death, spiritual illness, challenges of this life and the like.[3] Once the Law has been identified, the preacher can then speak of Christ, who not only fulfills the Law perfectly on our behalf, but also suffered, in our place, the punishment for breaking the Law so that we may be clean and holy in the eyes of God.

Preachers may also have challenges identifying the Gospel in a given text. The Gospel may appear within a text in different ways. Anytime there is Gospel, there is always going to be the God who, in His very nature, is the One who brings Good News to the hurting and healing to the brokenhearted. The preacher need only look for those instances when the relationship between God and man is made right. This could be the mention of a sacrifice or perhaps in the work of Jesus who brought the final sacrifice. There may also be instances in which creation itself is made "right" or "whole" again. Perhaps it is a mention of the "lion laying down with the lamb" or of some reversal of the original curse during the fall into sin. These examples are not merely the poetic license of speakers envisioning a different world. These instances are ones that occur only because Jesus has paid for the sin that occurred in the Garden and through that sacrifice promises a new heaven and a new earth. Such instances automatically name the actor: Jesus.

b) **The theme should be a declarative sentence.** One of the primary purposes of the theme sentence is to focus the thoughts of the preacher. It is unfortunate when such focusing occurs in retrospect, after the preacher preaches a sermon and has received critical feedback or has had time to ponder what he preached. It is much better for the preacher

---

3 For a good, brief discussion of different ways to see and approach the preaching of Law and Gospel in a text see Herman Stuempfle, *Preaching Law and Gospel* (Ramsey: Sigler Press, 1990), 17.

and the congregation to have such focus occur before the sermon is preached and even before the sermon is written

A primary trait of the theme sentence is that it should declare something. As Christians, we have a Gospel we believe, and we want to clearly confess that Gospel to all people. Many preachers will try to write theme sentences as questions. They believe this is a way to engage people. Unfortunately, such attempts do not engage congregations for lengths of time and also allow the sermon to degenerate into a situation where each person could have a different response. Questions also inherently lack the ability to confess what is believed or to make a truth statement about what the Church believes Christ is doing in this world. If the ultimate goal of preaching is to produce sermons in which people are given the opportunity to believe in Jesus and by believing have eternal life, then theme sentences comprised of a question are very poor at accomplishing this goal.

A theme sentence that actually declares something rather than asks a question will also challenge the preacher to be the kind of preacher who actually proclaims the Good News. Otherwise, he will risk becoming the type of preacher who slides into a morality tale rather than a matter of faith, viewing the sermon as merely a time for congregational self-improvement rather than comforting consciences. Take the example above from the raising of Lazarus, which says, "Jesus is calling people to believe and have eternal life in Him right now." This is quite a confession of faith. In addition to showing "Jesus" to be the actor, "Jesus" Himself is actually doing something: He is calling people to believe.

In addition to being a declarative sentence and one in which God is actively doing something, this simple sentence says quite a bit. First, because the verb is written in the present, active tense, it confesses that our God is active in the present world and at the present time. He is acting right here and right now. Second, the preacher is also confessing that our God is doing something. Our God is not a God who is sitting on a shelf somewhere gathering dust and watching history proceed on without Him. Our God is actively doing what our God does: bringing salvation to us. Third, the preacher is also confessing what we do in the Creed, that we believe our God is alive. Only a living God can be active and working salvation in the present tense. A dead God cannot do these things. The theme sentence is far more important than merely

83

focusing the thoughts of a preacher for linguistic reasons. It is a matter of faith. In one sentence, the preacher will be able to summarize a creedal confession of faith while at the same time specifically noting God's present activity based on the historic Scriptures . . . and all of this in just one sentence!

c) **The theme should help shape the sermon.** A good theme sentence is one that will clearly identify God's actions in the sermon and also declare a certain confession of faith. In addition to these benefits, the theme sentence also performs another helpful function for the preacher: it acts as a marker or guidepost throughout the sermon preparation and writing process.

It can be very easy for a preacher to lose his way when preparing or writing his sermon. What often occurs is that the preacher will have brought in an additional point that he may find interesting. For example, in one of our examples above, a theme sentence declared, "Jesus is calling people to believe and have eternal life in Him right now." Maybe while the preacher was writing his sermon, he began thinking about the Book of Revelation, which deals heavily with resurrection, and from there, he began thinking of all the people who are in heaven, and then he began to think about those who cried out and asked, "How long, oh, Lord?" He was so interested in this thought that the preacher ended up adding an entire paragraph to his sermon where he talked about these people waiting in heaven, took a few sentences to debunk beliefs like "purgatory" and then went back to the original theme about Jesus calling people in present life to believe and, in that believing, have eternal life.

Although these two themes have a similar connection (in that they are both dealing with eternal life in some way), the second theme is only tangentially related to the first. If the preacher were to bring in this additional theme, it would take the focus and attention off of the original theme and cause confusion amongst the congregation. When the preacher would try to return the congregation's thoughts back to his original theme, he would lose people. Some people may be able to make that leap but the majority would not, and they would be lost in thinking of creatures with eyes under their wings and people crying out under an altar. One of the main purposes in having a theme sentence is for that sentence to help shape the entire sermon writing process. By having a well-written theme sentence prior to the start of writing a sermon, the preacher has the ability to return to this theme sentence during his sermon writing to make sure that whatever content he is writing does indeed correspond with the respective theme sentence.

There is no doubt that theme sentences have the ability to direct a preacher's thoughts during the sermon-writing process. A good way to test the validity of this statement is to have ten different preachers write a theme sentence on the same passage and, once the theme sentence has been written, write a sermon based on his own theme sentence. Those ten different theme sentences will produce ten different sermons. There may indeed be similarities but some will undoubtedly be startlingly different from the others. Such an activity would show the positive influence a theme sentence can have in assisting the preacher in writing a well-focused sermon.

It is important for the preacher to understand that his theme sentence should not try to encompass every single thought or tidbit about a text. There will be other times to preach on other aspects of a text. The preacher should be comfortable in picking one singular theme and never straying from that singular theme throughout the sermon. Preachers may feel penned up by such construction, but the alternative is not worth it: hearers, when approached with too many themes or shifting themes, will stop listening. If hearers stop listening, they will fail to either hear the Gospel or to have their faith strengthened in this Jesus whom they heard about in the sermon. How truly sad to think that people would be denied the opportunity of hearing the Gospel for no other reason than a preacher was too undisciplined to organize his thoughts in a coherent manner.

Creating a sermon preparation worksheet is a vital part of writing a sermon. Far from simply being a worksheet that is completed with little to gain, this sheet encourages the preacher to think in theological terms about the biblical text and how it might be preached to a congregation. When most preachers think of the task of preaching, they usually believe that the majority of their time should be spent writing and perfecting the actual sermon. This should probably not be the case. Most preachers should spend the majority of their time working upon the development phases of writing a sermon rather than the actual writing itself. The "Sermon Preparation Worksheet" is one of those elements. The next chapter will present another developmental aspect that will greatly assist the preacher in actually writing his sermon.

OUT-OF-CLASS ASSIGNMENT

1. Students are to prepare a "theme sentence" as the final component of their Sermon Preparation Worksheet. Students should refer to the section above to note the components of a theme sentence as well as review the examples provided.

CHAPTER 13

THE LAW AND GOSPEL ARE FOR "YOU"

"And then from death awaken me. . . "

—*Lutheran Service Book*, #708, st. 3

As Christians, we only know of our history through the Bible. But even beyond that, we only know our theological history through the Bible. The Bible is far more than just a historical record book. We could and should say it is a record book of faith. The majority of the Old Testament stories do, in fact, tell a story of history, but they tell a greater story of believing or, as is the case perhaps more often, not believing (just read of the Israelites' fickle faith in Judges). As Christians, we have connectivity to the Scriptures that runs far deeper than just a record. It is a record of our unbelieving natures and of our God, who loved the unlovable so much that He came into our own flesh to bring believing back into creation.

Such a link should not be so easily discarded. Preachers should be very adamant in retaining connectivity to the Scriptures since it is by the written and then preached Word that people are able to believe and, by believing, have eternal life. To promote this connectivity, this primer will attempt to propose a simple and well-employed method of incorporating the Scriptures into a sermon. This will be done in such a way that the Scriptures retain their rightful place in our lives.

In order to teach this method, a metaphor will be employed that preachers can easily remember called "Five Pages." It is derived from a model that utilizes the Scriptures and our world, retaining a connection with the Scriptures in the hearer's life while encouraging continued belief.[1] In this metaphor, each of the "Five Pages" does not represent a real five-page sermon (although it could), but a movement within each page actually represents a larger movement within the sermon. They are broken down as follows: Page 1: Law in the text, Page 2: Law in our lives, Page 3: The Gospel in Christ, Page 4: Gospel in the text, Page 5: Gospel in our world. The final section of the "Sermon Preparation Worksheet" is to identify these five elements. Once they have been identified, then the actual sermon can be written.

Keeping such a tight connection between the text and our world is a simple way of keeping Christians and the Scriptures connected. This connectivity is far more than one Christian simply suggesting the Scriptures to someone "as a bit of good reading" or "because this is a really good book." Although the Scriptures may indeed be delightful reading, it is the fact that this is a book calling us back into a right relationship with God that makes the Bible the book that should be more closely connected to a Christian than the tefillin box was to the rabbi's head. The Scriptures are to be written within our very souls and are to be the Word of life to us. Just as Jesus told His disciples that He did not require food to eat, so also can the Christian be so filled with the certainty of his or her salvation in Christ that he or she will desire nothing else.

PAGE ONE

As the worksheet has already noted, the preacher will have selected a text and noted a single theme. These are huge milestones. Now it is time for the preacher to gather these two tightly related elements together and allow them the opportunity to speak further to God's people in the sermon. After reading the theme sentence once more, the preacher should read through the Scripture passage again. But before doing so, the preacher should have in the forefront of his mind two things: (1) The preacher has already identified what God is doing in this text. It will generally be a Gospel sentiment. The preacher should ask himself, "But why does God need to do this thing? Why

---

1   I offer complete credit to Paul Scott Wilson and his work *The Four Pages of the Sermon: A Guide to Biblical Preaching* (Nashville: Abingdon Press, 1999). The only significant alteration to his method is the proposed addition of a fifth page between pages 2 and 3. I deemed it necessary to add a section that speaks exclusively of Christ. Not that this was necessarily absent in the other pages, but I believe the move warranted a greater amount of devoted time.

is it that the people cannot do it for themselves, or the temple cannot do it for itself and the like?" and (2) the preacher should remember what the Law is, or better yet, what the Law does. The Law shows us that we are sinning. It shows us that by ourselves we cannot do what God has asked of us and, in fact, we actually run away from God and seek to trespass against God. That is what is in our heart of hearts, what sinning actually is.

Once the preacher has considered these two elements, he should read the text. After doing a run-through of the text, the preacher should write down at least 3 to 5 examples of Law that are within the text. It is important the preacher not stray from the text at this point. Once the preacher has written down several examples of the Law, the preacher should see which ones are most applicable to the identified theme. In other words, examples of the Law should show why the theme sentence is needed. Sometimes it can be challenging to find the Law. In this case, the preacher should reread his theme sentence one more time and ask himself again, "Why does God need to do this?" This should help the preacher identify the Law within the text. After the preacher has identified an example of the Law that matches the theme sentence in content, he should write a one-sentence statement on his "Sermon Preparation Worksheet" summarizing the Law in the Scriptures. This would be the beginning of the metaphorical "first page."

Take time to write down the law portions that came to mind in your Sermon Preparation Worksheet. These should be examples of the law within the text. Then note which ones especially match up with the theme sentence.

Page Two

Our lives should never be separated from the Scriptures. And indeed, the sins people struggled with in the Scriptures are the same ones people are struggling with today. There is nothing new under the sun. The Virgin Mary found herself to be an unwed mother and undoubtedly heard whispers behind her back. Peter did not turn out to be the "rock" of faith his name implies. Paul may have brought the faith to the Gentiles but he also oversaw the killing of Stephen. The saints of old are true examples for us of how to live in the faith, but they are also examples of sinful natures just like ours. Whether it is before or even after their conversions, they still struggled with their sinful flesh and still needed to hear and believe Christ's Word in Absolution for them.

Preaching the Law well can be the most challenging aspect of preaching. As stated, it takes great effort for preachers to understand how they are sinning much less how others are. There may indeed be times when preachers can and should preach in an accusatory manner. Sometimes they must be faithful to their calling and bring before the congregation's eyes the sins they or their church are committing by flat out telling them. But the greatest challenges and a more lasting preaching of the Law is when the preacher assists hearers in seeing for themselves the laws they are trespassing. For example, when a crowd accused a woman of adultery, Jesus never said to them, "All of you have broken the Sixth Commandment just like her!" or some other accusatory remark. On the contrary, Jesus simply said, "Let him who is without sin among you be the first to throw a stone at her."[2] The Law Jesus preached in that moment, in that one sentence, was some of the greatest Law preached. It was not accusatory. Jesus' Words allowed the people to mull over what He said for themselves. The Word that was preached is what condemned the people. Jesus had every right to tell them they were sinning and to stop. He was the only One who rightfully could. But even He didn't. He allowed the Holy Spirit to convict the people of their sin. This is the type of Law that preachers should strive to emulate in their preaching.

To recognize the sin in the lives of a preacher's congregation, he must know his congregation. A shepherd must know his sheep or he is a poor shepherd and mere hired hand. This occurs not only by talking to people but by listening to them. He should hear their struggles and help bear their burdens in a non-judgmental fashion. Based on the text, the preacher also has a window into the "public" sins of the past with which our own forefathers in the faith struggled. We are no different from them.

Once the preacher has considered his congregation and the direction the Law gives in the text, he should look for similar instances of sinning that occur in the present. Preachers should steer away from preaching a bland Law that throws a handful of darts at a board in the hope of hitting someone and should instead anticipate what are the types of sin their parishioners are committing and experiencing.

It can be very freeing for congregational members to hear the sins that they struggle with mentioned specifically in a sermon. It allows them to

---

2   John 8:7 (ESV).

realize that although their sins are terrible, even "it" can be forgiven by Christ. For this reason, preachers should not shy away from considering the sins that people may struggle with, even if they are never uttered from the mouth of a parishioner. Doing so may allow a parishioner the chance to see a long struggle with sin spoken of, so that there might be the chance for the Gospel. As with the previous page, once the preacher has had time to consider, he should write down three to five examples and select a one-sentence summary that he can include on his "Sermon Preparations Worksheet." Once he has identified this, he can write that sentence on his worksheet and the "Second Page" will be complete.

Students should now take note of the Law in the world around us and in the lives of the congregation. That may seem like a wide task, but this is where the theme sentence and "Page 1: Law" will aid the preacher. By now, a clear direction will have formed allowing the preacher to identify specific examples of Law occurring in the lives of the congregation directly related to the text.

PAGE THREE

"In the beginning was the Word. And the Word was with God, and the Word was God" (John 1:1). Jesus, that one Word, was there in Eden. He was there reassuring Noah to continue believing. He was there calling Abraham to step out and abandon all things and believe in a new life He was giving. That Word rose throughout history not just in the record of the Scriptures, but in the lives of the people. Paper does not believe; people do. And it is only through the Scriptures, only through the Word, that we have the opportunity to see Jesus through the eyes of John, who was a witness to that Light. Through the Scriptures, we have the opportunity to see Jesus through John's eyes and hear through his ears. Through him and the other witnesses of the faith, we have been given the opportunity to hear them speak back to us what God first spoke to them. As the Scriptures say, "The law was given through Moses, but grace and truth came through Jesus Christ."[3] This is why the preacher has a great task in his sermon preparation.

At this point, the preacher has identified the Law. People have seen and are deliberating for themselves on their sinfulness toward God as well as

---

3   John 1.

their dire need for Him. During this section of the "Sermon Preparation Worksheet," the preacher should also note the actions of Jesus. In many ways, these will already be self-evident through the theme sentence, which is geared toward an action that God is doing. Now the preacher has a chance specifically to state this based upon the text. By looking though this text, the preacher should ask, "What exactly is Jesus doing? What is He saying? How is He moving?" We do not move from Law to Gospel without Jesus. There is no fulfillment of the Law without Jesus.

At this point, it is also very easy for preachers to turn into prosperity preachers. As sinful humans, we are always tempted to forego the reason why Jesus came in our flesh. He suffered in our place so that we could be released from our sins, died in our place for the forgiveness and removal of those sins and then came to new life through physical resurrection for our sakes. All of this is for us! All of this is to rectify the fall into sin that occurred in Eden. The preacher should never shy away from this in his proclamation of the Gospel for it is by this that people hear, believe and are saved. Preachers will always be tempted to soften Jesus, to make Him a friendlier or more approachable Jesus. They may make Him into a Jesus who is indeed a bread king who just serves soup to those who are hungry or the Jesus who loves to live in political rallies and supports certain parties. But that is not the kingdom of Jesus. Judas made this mistake, Simon believed in this mistake and the crowds bought into this mistake. We, as Lutherans, should always pray and confess in our preaching that "God's kingdom comes when our heavenly Father gives us His Holy Spirit, so that by His grace we believe His holy Word and lead godly lives here in time and there in eternity."[4]

Preachers should pray not to fall into the sin of Adam and Eve (Satan's sin), trying to reshape God into our image and our likeness. Our God is who He is. He is the only One who can claim the great name of "I AM," the One who exists in and of Himself with no assistance or reliance on others. This is the God preachers are called to preach. Preachers may yearn for a different Jesus, a more exciting Jesus, a Jesus who does what they want, a Jesus who is more "applicable" in some way to the people. But that is not who our God is, and we do not dictate to God how God is to act, let alone be. God reveals Himself to us only through the Scriptures, and through the Scriptures, we preachers gaze through the eyes of all witnesses who experience His grace, kindness and undeserved love. Through the preaching

---

4 *Small Catechism*, p. 20.

of the Gospel, preachers allow themselves and others to believe what our fathers and mothers in the faith have seen and heard as if we have seen with our own eyes and heard with our own ears because really we have.

Perhaps this is why Luther said that in some ways the sermon was greater than the Scriptures.[5] He did not mean this when it came to authority over faith and life. What he meant is that through preaching the Word of God continues to live and continues to call people to believe.

Using his theme sentence as the guide, the preacher should survey the Law and the text and then clearly state in one sentence exactly who is speaking to rescue the people from the judgment of the Law. Preachers should try not to speak in abstractions, reverting to the same few sentences about the cross. Preachers will always return to the event that saved the cosmos. But this should be done every time with new eyes, turning around this salvation event and gazing at it through different lenses like one could turn and view a diamond. There are different eyes through which to see salvation, from the women, to the men, to the children. There is a multitude of ways to see, enjoy and speak the salvation of Christ for all people. The preacher is called to identify that Law, speak to that Law through this connectivity of Jesus Christ Himself and then move toward spending time with the hearers in the speaking of the Gospel.

By now the Law has been identified. But the only way to heal the breaking of the Law is through the sacrifice of Jesus. During this page, students will be encouraged to engage why it was that Jesus intervened in this world to save us from the breaking of this specific Law that was raised. This could be a short section or a longer one, but Christ must be present in order to advance to the Gospel, which He alone is by His very nature.

Fourth Page

There is a simple reason why preachers incorporate the Scriptures so much into their sermons and don't speak of their own thoughts. It is within the Scriptures that we learn that, because of the fall, we have lost any innate ability to know, understand or come to a knowledge of God's own goodness

---

5   "There is greater power in the testament than in the sacrament; for a man can have and use the word or testament apart from the sign or sacrament . . . for I can set the words of Christ before me and with them feed and strengthen my faith as often as I choose" (Luther, *Word and Sacrament II*, 44.)

or mercy predisposed toward us. It is not within us to believe the Gospel. It is only God's goodness shown to us through Christ that we know anything of the Gospel. And it is only through the Scriptures that we come to know of that goodness in Christ. The Scriptures build upon God's first great proc-lamation of the Gospel to Adam and Eve, which foreshadowed Christ. In that moment, the memory that creation had lost through its trespass was brought to mind again; sinners would become sinless again, not through their own actions but by the mercy of God. This mercy was originally known by creation but was abandoned to embrace Satan's lie. And yet, through this Gospel, God brought His people back to Him. It was His choice and His action, not our own.

Ever since Eden, God respoke His Word of goodness and love to His cre-ation. Out of that first Gospel, the prophets were inspired and the Gospel grew until it finally culminated in the final and fullest Word: Jesus Christ Himself. The past 2,000 years have seen the Christian Church continue to build on the foundation of Jesus' original Gospel Words, as we march toward the final eschaton both individually and corporately as the Body of Christ. During this time, Christians hear the Gospel not only in the Scriptures and liturgy, but the Words themselves do the action, bringing hearers to faith and releasing them from their sins. This is meant in a far different manner than in some form of ceremonial witchcraft or in the belief that the mere speaking of words causes change. The Gospel comes only from God, and it is from God's pronouncement of freedom and God's pronouncement of our release from our trespassing that anyone has the chance to believe that they are indeed free. Preaching is one such vehicle for God's way of creating believing.

For the preacher, it is vital that we allow hearers to see the free reign of the Gospel in this world. The reign begins in the Scriptures. The Scriptures are our records of believing and not believing. If we are going to point out the Law and the trespasses that people committed in the Scriptures, then we must likewise show them the salvation that Christ bestowed upon them in the Scriptures. God never abandons His people. It is vital for preachers to use their theme statement (which is essentially Gospel based) and find the very clear outpouring of the Gospel within the sermon text.

God does not abandon His creation. Page 4 is about showing how Jesus rescues His people from sin, death and the devil in the scriptures. During this page, the preacher should return to his theme sentence and use it throughout his sermon planning and future writing.

The Fifth Page

The final page to be constructed for the sermon is the fifth page. Up to this point, the preacher has identified the Law in the text and in the lives of the congregation. The preacher has shared Christ through the third page as the only One capable of saving people from their sin. The preacher then did due diligence in returning to the Gospel so that the congregation could see and hear how God saves all His people from their sins, including those within the biblical text. Now, the preacher is called to speak that same Word of freedom to his own congregation here in the present.

In speaking the Gospel to his congregation at this point in time, the preacher should be cautious not to throw to the proverbial wind everything that he has worked so hard in creating. The preacher should retrace his footsteps, starting with his theme sentence and then look down the path of Law and Gospel already laid out for him. The specific Gospel that is to be shared with his congregation at this point in time will mirror and reflect the Law and Gospel already spoken.

In many homiletical traditions, this section of the sermon is the most vital. In the African American preaching tradition, they often identify this section as "celebration," a time in which the entire congregation truly celebrates the salvation Christ has given them. This occurs via the preacher who acts as the mouthpiece of the congregation as they together relish the good things Christ is doing for them in their lives and the hope He has given them, a hope beyond measure, unmerited and full of undeserved love and goodness.

Lutherans have tended to view this section (i.e., the Gospel) as the greatest pinnacle of the sermon. It is for this reason alone that preachers preach. They preach so that people might hear the Gospel and by believing have eternal life. The preaching of the Law is simply necessary in order to preach the Gospel. It is only through the devastation of our souls through the Law that we become a barren landscape. And it is through the preaching of the Gospel that a garden of life in Christ is planted within that barrenness. The

95

Gospel is simply not as sweet without first being reminded of the tartness of the Law.

But why should Lutherans do this? If preaching the Gospel in the sermon is the true goal of preaching, why not just go straight to this part of the sermon? This will be a temptation for many preachers. Preachers have the same fallen flesh as all other people, and it is within our sinful natures that we desire to overlook our sins and wickedness in this world, even overlooking our disobedience toward God. We long for only sunny days and candies. But that is an illusion. This world has fallen; it is not perfect. Anyone who fails to preach the Law has decided to live within the illusion created by Satan during the fall. This person has no place in preaching the Gospel before God's people and should carefully consider Paul's words to Timothy before undertaking the preaching of the Gospel as a vocation (1 Timothy 5; 2 Timothy 4).

But for those who do preach the Law, this section of preaching the Gospel is truly the end goal and the sweetest part of the sermon. For this reason, the Gospel should predominate. Some have argued that the Gospel can be simply a few sentences at the end of a sermon and thereby strike people by the novelty and overpowering of such short, decisive words. But this is not the case. The Gospel should predominate not only in the quality of speech but also in the quantity of speech. A little over half of the sermon should be Gospel so that people might truly hear and believe Jesus, and by believing have eternal life in Him.

This raises another common temptation for preachers during this section of the sermon: they will be tempted to mingle Law and Gospel or attempt to put a pretty face on the ugly Law to make it look like the beautiful Gospel. When proclaiming the Gospel, it should be unhindered by the ugliness of the Law. The Gospel should be radical in that it stands alone and is not propped up by our abilities or will, just as Paul encouraged the Galatians in their own preaching (Gal. 3:1). For example, imagine a preacher is near the end of the sermon. His sermon was based on the portion of the Beatitudes that said, "Blessed are the poor in spirit for theirs is the kingdom of heaven." A very poor mingling of Law and Gospel could look like this:

> "Even though you are poor, you do own the kingdom of heaven. God has given it to you. So, now it is up to you to go out and pay off that debt to God. Be kind to your neighbors to pay back God. Be gracious to your family to pay back God. Be

faithful to Him to pay back God."

The first sentence in this example is Gospel. It is Good News that we own the kingdom of heaven that God has given us. However, the preacher has taken that free gift God has given and has now placed a law and burden back upon the hearers by telling them that they must now go out and do something to "pay back God." Either a gift is a true gift, meaning it is free and freely given from one to another (Gospel), or that "gift" is something earned in which someone must work for it and if he has not worked enough or earned enough, he will fail to receive the payment (Law).

However, the preacher could treat that same passage with a Gospel approach by saying,

> Even though you are poor, you do own the kingdom of heaven. God has given it to you. You never could have paid enough to God; you don't have enough. You never could have been kind enough to your neighbors; that wouldn't be enough. You could never be good enough to your family; that wouldn't ever pay for it. And your faithfulness to God, as sincere as it may be, will never be wealthy enough for God. It is because of Christ that you receive this gift, and it is through Christ that you came to be certain you really do own the kingdom of heaven, because Christ has done what is needed for you to have it, and He gives it to you.

In this example, there is no mingling of the Law and the Gospel. In fact, it is just the opposite. The hearer is reminded that he can do nothing to merit God's worthiness. This fact is reinforced very clearly by the final sentence in which the hearer's hope is squarely centered on Christ and Christ alone. The final section of the sermon must be clear and sharp in its declaration that salvation comes freely from Jesus.

Page 5 emphasizes purely the Gospel to the congregation. It will mirror the theme sentence and be its final fulfillment at the congregational level. Make sure that this Gospel is accomplished by God alone and that the congregation knows it is "for you." After Page 5 has been completed, the preacher should be encouraged to go ahead and assemble the 5 pages together into the actual sermon. They may choose to do this by writing it word for word, or by writing in an outline format. Either way, the student will be well prepared with their 5 pages worksheet.

CHAPTER 14

RETURNING TO THE SERMON

"Return to the Lord your God, for He is gracious and merciful."

—Joel 2:13

"Should a preacher write his sermon, or should the preacher just walk into the pulpit with absolutely no preparation? Perhaps the preacher should place a few notes down on a piece of paper, or maybe it is better the preacher have just a few thoughts formed in his head before stepping into the pulpit." This is one of the first questions preachers will ask. At face value, there is nothing inherently wrong with any of these approaches. The benefit of writing out a sermon is that the preacher can see what he is going to say. This allows preachers the time to go back to his sermon, making sure Law and Gospel are spoken correctly. Preachers need to make sure they deliver their sermon in a fresh style, as if spoken for the first time, but this can be taught over time with practice.

Preachers who choose to write out a few words or enter the pulpit with a few thoughts have done well in that they generally know where they will be going in their sermon, but they run the risk of failing to remember how those thoughts interconnect. Spontaneity may not be a concern, but content is.

The preacher who chooses no preparation but just walks into the pulpit unprepared is of a concern on many levels. From a practical level, the preacher has not prepared for his sermon. He does not know what he will speak. This is evident in the meandering styles of such preachers who repeat themselves and often stumble around their words and thoughts like drunk men. Theologically, there could be concerns as well. Perhaps this preacher does not believe that he has a sinful flesh that, through prayer and meditation, must be beaten down, especially with such a pure task entrusted to him as preaching the Gospel to the congregation. Such a man can also be subject to arrogance and may draw attention to himself, especially if he likes to walk around in a dramatic fashion. He draws eyes to himself and not to Christ. This is a form of idolatry; the preacher has made himself one to be adored and not the One of whom he speaks.

This primer was written with the encouragement to have students either write out their sermon fully or prepare their sermons in some type of outline format if they are capable of speaking in such a way. (Over the years, I have seen few preachers able to master this format successfully and master it well so that the Gospel is still proclaimed and good content is presented to the people.)

One of the greatest benefits to writing out a sermon is that the preacher can return to that sermon. He can prayerfully consider what he has written to determine that it is a good Word from God. This may involve returning to the Scriptures for study or consulting trusted and respected brother pastors. In fact, returning to the sermon that has already been written also possesses its own steps for reviewing. The following chapter will propose a few elements to consider when reviewing a sermon prior to preaching.

Does God Remain the Actor?

Modern computers can aid the preacher a great deal in this task (although reading through a text won't take that long either). This step is rather simple: locate all the instances in your sermon in which "God" has been named. This may be challenging in some cases because "God" may have been spoken as "Jesus" or the "Holy Spirit" or maybe as the "Creator." Once these instances have been identified, simply look to how God is spoken of grammatically. If God is simply spoken of in the predicate of the sentence, if He is referenced purely in passing or if He is mentioned merely as a passive actor, then changes should be considered. (Incidentally, this is one good reason to write out a sermon fully—much easier to review to ensure good Gospel is being proclaimed!) Most of the instances in which "God" is mentioned should immediately attach an active verb to that name for "God." An example of speaking of God in a passive fashion could be this:

When you look into your hearts, think about God. Remember all the times during your day when you think about Him.

In this example, "God" is purely a passive noun; He is just sitting there doing nothing. The actor in this example would actually be the person. Here's another:

> Think about your offerings of time, talent and treasure. What can you give to God? You have worked hard, you put in eight hours a day, you drive kids to school, you make dinner, you clean the house. You do it all. That is some hard work. Now it is time to give back. And the first one to receive your offerings should be God.

In this example, "God" is merely the recipient of an action a hearer would be performing. God is passive, just sitting there. In fact, if this were not spoken of within a Christian church, these statements could easily be spoken of by a Muslim, Jew or Hindu. It could be very easy to consider a hardworking Hindu man coming to bring a bowl of milk as an offering to this god so he wouldn't somehow starve! Christianity is different from every other world religion in that God remains the actor and bringer of salvation and does so independent of any help from created creatures. In fact, while we were still sinners and in opposition to God, He chose to bring salvation to us.[1]

CHECKING THE SERMON:

1. Locate all the instances in which "God" is mentioned in the sermon.

2. Is God actually doing something (active) or is He merely receiving something from the hearer (passive)?

3. Although some passive references may be fine, try changing passive references to God into active ones in which God is the bringer of judgment, salvation, healing, forgiveness and the like.

4. Ensure that the Gospel sections of the sermon feature God as the actor and that the verbs show God as the doer of an action.

5. Check your references to "God." Is "Christ" specifically mentioned as the bringer of salvation?

---

1   Romans 5:8.

Does the Gospel Remain Pure?

While noting if God is the actor, spoken of in the active or passive tense, also note what the person's relationship to God is in that scenario. A preacher can do this by first noticing where the instances of "God" are spoken and then looking in close proximity to the instances in which the "hearer" is mentioned in relation to God. Then, pay close attention to how "God" and "man" interact. Is "man" doing something for "God?" Is "man" relying upon "God" or is "God" relying upon "man?" An example could be something like this:

> When was the last time you praised God? When was it? Last week? Last night? Or was it last Christmas when you came to church? When was the last time you praised God? God loves our praises. God takes in those praises as offerings to Him. Without that praise, without that worship given to Him, our God is hurt. He needs your praises. And if those praises don't go up to Him, then the blessings won't come down.

There are many problems with the above example. God is not "hurt" by the lack of praise in the sense of being wounded as to be weakened. God also does not "need" our praise; although God receives the prayers of His saints as a sweet aroma, He won't somehow starve if they are not given. In fact, He did just fine before creating man. A preacher should never portray God as a spoiled child who won't give something to you unless you first give something to Him.

But the overarching challenge, aside from the examples just provided, is that the actions in this example were all completed by man. God was not doing anything, and as such, there was no Gospel. The Gospel is inherently God's action of saving us through Christ. The Gospel is not a concentration on the works of man toward God. It is very easy for preachers to fall into this trap. We sinners are very adept at dressing up the Law to make it look pretty enough to maybe pass as the Gospel. But the saying holds true, "You can put a pig in a pretty dress, but you're still left with a pig in a pretty dress." No matter how a preacher dresses up the Law, it is still the Law and condemns us of our sin. The Gospel must be free from the actions of man, remaining pure. This purity is achieved only when the works of God are completed for us through Christ and are never left hanging out in the air as if God has chosen to bring salvation through another vessel (namely us). God was pleased to have salvation dwell within His Son and achieved that salvation through Him alone.

CHECKING THE SERMON:

1. Find the times when "God" is mentioned in relation to "man."

2. In those instances, is "man" doing something for "God" (remember the pig in a dress) or is God doing something for man (Gospel)?

3. Look for other instances in which the hearers of the sermon are mentioned in the sermon.

4. Are the hearers active in "doing" something for God (active), or do they remain the receivers of the good things God has done for them (passive)?

5. Are the actions completed by "God" done through "Christ," or was the sermon left open as if there could be another vessel (us) that could somehow wrongly be placed with the burden of bringing salvation?

THIS IS FOR "YOU"

The culmination of the sermon should be to move hearers toward the metaphorical "third page" of the sermon where they meet Jesus Christ Himself in His Word. The sermon should lend itself toward Gospel proclamation for the remaining "two pages" of the five-page model. Many preachers will find it very challenging to speak the Gospel for at least 50 percent of their sermon. Granted, there will be appropriate times when the preacher will need to deviate, but this Gospel predominance should be normative.[2]

Another noteworthy element of this Gospel section (which can also, at times, be found during the Law section) is that the hearer is to know and hear and believe for himself that the Gospel is for him. What this means is that the preacher actually needs to say in his sermon that this message is "for you." Preachers should never forget that the Good News of being saved

---

2   Few protestant denominations are comfortable with speaking the Gospel for a prolonged period of time in a sermon. It seems counterintuitive, but this is essentially an accepted principle (see Paul Scott Wilson, *The Four Pages of the Sermon*). For a worthy discussion about extending the time spent on proclamation see Henry Mitchell's *Celebration and Experience in Preaching* (Nashville: Abingdon Press, 1990).

in Christ is meant to be received by living and breathing people. Preachers should also not assume that people will just "get it" when the preacher talks about "some" Good News that is in Christ. No, the preacher has a duty, responsibility and calling to tell people that this Good News is "for you." To do otherwise would restrict Christ in His incarnational work of coming into this world as the preached Word. To fail to deliver the Gospel into people's ears by telling them this is really "for you" would confine Christ to a box and not allow Him to interact with creation. Some examples of Gospel written "for you" are as follows:

> Christ was serious when He shared that last meal with His disciples. Christ was so serious He called it His last will and testament. They were dying words from a man who would soon be nailed on a cross for the forgiveness of all of His disciples' sins and for the forgiveness of all of your sins.

Another example that highlights how the Gospel is "for you" the hearer but without stating it so obviously is a way of enrolling people into the biblical or Gospel story. An example taken from the same biblical event is as follows:

> The disciples reclined at the table with Jesus. He said this was His last meal with them. Then Jesus said that the bread they were breaking was His body and the cup they were drinking was His blood. Today, on this Maundy Thursday evening, it is hard not to see ourselves at that same table as Jesus feeds you with His body and as the cup is passed. It is the same sacrifice, given and shed for the forgiveness of all of our sins.

Identifying that the Gospel is "for you" is not a means of encouraging some type of individualistic Christianity any more than the Words of Institution and distribution of the Supper would.[3] Rather, the Gospel is meant to be received, taken in and believed by "you," the hearer. Jesus Christ saved all of creation because He loves what His hand has created and desires to cradle that creation once more. This happens when creatures believe that Christ's gracious work was for them. To preach in any other manner would inad-

---

3   The common Words of Institution say, ". . . take, eat, this is My body, which is given **for you** . . . take, drink, this cup is the New Testament which is shed **for you**." And, during distribution pastors will often say, "Take and eat, this is the true body of our Lord and Savior Jesus Christ, given into death **for you** for the forgiveness of all of your sins . . . take and drink, this is the true blood of our Lord and Savior Jesus Christ, shed **for you** for the forgiveness of all of your sins."

vertently separate Christ and His creation; it would prevent creation from believing in its God who saved it and would mirror Satan's original work in the Garden of Eden in separating God and man from one another. That sin had enormous reverberations through creation. But through the speaking of the Gospel of Christ for "you," the hearer, those ripples can stop.

CHECKING THE SERMON

1. Find the Gospel sentences in your sermon.

2. Check to see if those sentences speak of the Gospel in abstract terms as if it is something someone is watching or if the preacher is engaging the hearer by the actions of the Gospel (this would be the difference between watching soccer on TV as opposed to being on the field and actually playing soccer.)

3. Identify what Gospel words are used to engage the audience, allowing them to be "on the field." This can be done by simply seeing if there are times when the Gospel is said to be "for you" or if the hearer is some-one enveloped in that Gospel by some other means.

4. Locate the sections in the sermon that center upon the preaching of the Law.

5. As with the Gospel sections, see what words are used to engage hearers in the preaching of the Law. The Law was written not for itself; it was written to convict all of us of our sin.

IS THE INCARNATION CONCRETE OR ABSTRACT?

Sometimes theologically weighty elements can be changed by how we speak of them. Take, for example, the following two examples. The first offers a weak way of speaking about Absolution while the second is stronger:

> "Sometimes we don't always feel forgiven; we can feel like the sin is still with us. We can think that the sin won't go away. It can seem like nothing will ever change. But over time, we hope Jesus will take those worries away."

Now, from a theological standpoint, there was nothing necessarily wrong with this section. Everything stated is true and right. But just because it is true and right does not mean it is incarnational. The Old Testament was true and right, but it lacked Christ and did not find its fulfillment until the coming of Christ (Gal. 4:4). In addition, the words I used did not possess a very incarnational quality to them. The words "feel" and "think" and "seem" are all "head" words; you can't reach out and touch "think" or "feel." Even within this example, Jesus Himself held nothing more than a phantomlike presence among us. He was a character, but He was not living and breathing and touching. The incarnation is sometimes raw and gritty and all around us. You can reach out and touch the incarnation, just as Thomas and the other apostles did. Our speech should follow a similar pattern. Consider the next example with those elements reversed:

> "Sometimes we don't feel forgiven. We can see the look our husband or wife still gives us. We look at our own hands and hearts and see them as never being clean enough; no soap is capable of washing that sin off of us. Working in an office building, people sometimes think they know your life better than you do yourself. At times, we may as well have the word "sinner" tattooed across our forehead because that is what people see and it is how dirty we feel. But then today, a divine hand touched your head, a divine hand placed bread in your mouth, a divine hand cupped itself around your ear as Jesus whispered, "Do you believe I can forgive your sin?" And with weak responses that we can barely muster, sometimes not understanding the fullness of it ourselves, we whisper with hope, "Yes, I believe that You are the Christ, the Son of the living God." And in your ear and into your heart, Jesus says, "I forgive you all your sins in My name." In that moment you are not the same. You are not the same person. You will never be the same person again, because now, you are forgiven by Jesus Himself."

These two examples offer startling differences. In general, the language is more concrete. An example of how the sin is still with us was shown in the words "we can still see the look our husband or wife gives us." In general, it is best to show rather than tell when it comes to preaching.

CONCLUSION

The Word truly is becoming flesh and dwelling among us and within us still today. There is no higher calling than speaking the Gospel. This is what was first entrusted to Adam, who shared that Word with Eve, and they together passed the *protoevangelium* down the lines. But as always with the Word from God, the devil despises it and constantly attacks those who speak it, whether it is a Gospel spoken within the home or within a congregation. As preachers who have begun their task, you have been given a high calling by your church and from God Himself. Preserve yourself in this calling through humility and by studying the Scriptures and the catechism. Guard how and what you preach. Plant the seed among the people, and allow God to work through the Holy Spirit, never knowing the wonderful seed that may grow.

This primer is a first step for some or perhaps a review for others. It was not designed to answer the complex questions that often arise after years of preaching, but it seeks to establish a theological foundation for preaching. It also attempted to provide a framework for students to engage the biblical text in a Lutheran way in order to promote the Gospel within a biblical text. Other topics like preaching to the twenty-first-century mind, the construction of a distinctively Lutheran sermon, how preachers might preach simply about the ever-increasing presence of sexual sins in the modern world will have to wait for a different time.

+ Now may the grace of our Lord Jesus Christ, the love of God and the communion of the Holy Spirit be with you as you open your mouth and speak that creative Word first spoken in creation and now respoken by our Lord, Jesus Christ, through you. Amen. +

APPENDIX

SERMON PREPARATION WORKSHEETS

SERMON PREPARATION WORKSHEET

Text:_____

God Is the Actor _____

    What is God doing or wanting to do through this text?

    State the action of God in one sentence.

    How is God presently acting in this world according to this text?

Jesus Is Our Redeemer _____

    How does this text point us to Jesus for salvation?

    How was the Gospel written for "you?"

    How can or should the congregation see themselves in this text?

    How can the sermon be preached so people believe the Gospel is for them?

The Holy Spirit Works Faith _____

    When are people encouraged to believe in the works of God?

    When are people encouraged to believe in God / Jesus Himself?

    Are there times when the "for you" section points to tangible events? If not, how could that be strengthened?

Theme sentence_____

Sermon Preparation Worksheet:
Law and Gospel

Page 1

- Identify 3-5 examples of "Law" within this biblical text.
- Note those examples that complement your theme sentence.

Page 2

- Identify similar Law examples in the present world.
- Which commandment would be broken if this Law were not kept?
- Are there times your sheep (congregation) also break this Law? Is this a law people take pleasure in breaking? Do people feel guilty when breaking this Law? Would people feel that God is angry when this Law is broken?

Page 3

- Why would Jesus become involved in saving people from this particular sin?
- How does Jesus' death and resurrection save people from this particular sin?

Page 4

- What are the ways that you see your theme sentence affecting the biblical scene?
- How is Jesus bringing Gospel to this biblical scene?
- If an Old Testament or Epistle passage, how is Christ involved in this Bible story?

Page 5

- How does your theme sentence show the Gospel in this present world?
- In what ways are you allowing the congregation believe they have a new life in Christ?
- Have you stated that this Gospel is truly "for you" the hearer?

Sermon Preparation Worksheet

Text:_____

God Is the Actor _____

    What is God doing or wanting to do through this text?

    State the action of God in one sentence.

    How is God presently acting in this world according to this text?

Jesus Is Our Redeemer _____

    How does this text point us to Jesus for salvation?

    How was the Gospel written for "you?"

    How can or should the congregation see themselves in this text?

    How can the sermon be preached so people believe the Gospel is
    for them?

The Holy Spirit Works Faith _____

    When are people encouraged to believe in the works of God?

    When are people encouraged to believe in God / Jesus Himself?

    Are there times when the "for you" section points to tangible
    events? If not, how could that be strengthened?

Theme sentence_____

SERMON PREPARATION WORKSHEET: LAW AND GOSPEL

Page 1

- Identify 3-5 examples of "Law" within this biblical text.
- Note those examples that complement your theme sentence.

Page 2

- Identify similar Law examples in the present world.
- Which commandment would be broken if this Law were not kept?
- Are there times your sheep (congregation) also break this Law? Is this a people take pleasure in breaking? Do people feel guilty when breaking this Law? Would people feel that God is angry when this Law is broken?

Page 3

- Why would Jesus become involved in saving people from this particular sin?
- How does Jesus' death and resurrection save people from this particular sin?

Page 4

- What are the ways that you see your theme sentence affecting the biblical scene?
- How is Jesus bringing Gospel to this biblical scene?
- If an Old Testament or Epistle passage, how is Christ involved in this Bible story?

Page 5

- How does your theme sentence show the Gospel in this present world?
- In what ways are you allowing the congregation believe they have a new life in Christ?
- Have you stated that this Gospel is truly "for you" the hearer?

Sermon Preparation Worksheet

Text:_____

God Is the Actor _____

    What is God doing or wanting to do through this text?

    State the action of God in one sentence.

    How is God presently acting in this world according to this text?

Jesus Is Our Redeemer _____

    How does this text point us to Jesus for salvation?

    How was the Gospel written for "you?"

    How can or should the congregation see themselves in this text?

    How can the sermon be preached so people believe the Gospel is for them?

The Holy Spirit Works Faith _____

    When are people encouraged to believe in the works of God?

    When are people encouraged to believe in God / Jesus Himself?

    Are there times when the "for you" section points to tangible events? If not, how could that be strengthened?

Theme sentence_____

SERMON PREPARATION WORKSHEET:
LAW AND GOSPEL

Page 1

- Identify 3-5 examples of "Law" within this biblical text.
- Note those examples that complement your theme sentence.

Page 2

- Identify similar Law examples in the present world.
- Which commandment would be broken if this Law were not kept?
- Are there times your sheep (congregation) also break this Law? Is this a law people take pleasure in breaking? Do people feel guilty when breaking this Law? Would people feel that God is angry when this Law is broken?

Page 3

- Why would Jesus become involved in saving people from this particular sin?
- How does Jesus' death and resurrection save people from this particular sin?

Page 4

- What are the ways that you see your theme sentence affecting the biblical scene?
- How is Jesus bringing Gospel to this biblical scene?
- If an Old Testament or Epistle passage, how is Christ involved in this Bible story?

Page 5

- How does your theme sentence show the Gospel in this present world?
- In what ways are you allowing the congregation believe they have a new life in Christ?
- Have you stated that this Gospel is truly "for you" the hearer?

Sermon Preparation Worksheet

Text:_____

God Is the Actor _____

    What is God doing or wanting to do through this text?

    State the action of God in one sentence.

    How is God presently acting in this world according to this text?

Jesus Is Our Redeemer _____

    How does this text point us to Jesus for salvation?

    How was the Gospel written for "you?"

    How can or should the congregation see themselves in this text?

    How can the sermon be preached so people believe the Gospel is for them?

The Holy Spirit Works Faith _____

    When are people encouraged to believe in the works of God?

    When are people encouraged to believe in God / Jesus Himself?

    Are there times when the "for you" section points to tangible events? If not, how could that be strengthened?

Theme sentence_____

Sermon Preparation Worksheet: Law and Gospel

Page 1

- Identify 3-5 examples of "Law" within this biblical text.
- Note those examples that complement your theme sentence.

Page 2

- Identify similar Law examples in the present world.
- Which commandment would be broken if this Law were not kept?
- Are there times your sheep (congregation) also break this Law? Is this a law people take pleasure in breaking? Do people feel guilty when breaking this Law? Would people feel that God is angry when this Law is broken?

Page 3

- Why would Jesus become involved in saving people from this particular sin?
- How does Jesus' death and resurrection save people from this particular sin?

Page 4

- What are the ways that you see your theme sentence affecting the biblical scene?
- How is Jesus bringing Gospel to this biblical scene?
- If an Old Testament or Epistle passage, how is Christ involved in this Bible story?

Page 5

- How does your theme sentence show the Gospel in this present world?
- In what ways are you allowing the congregation believe they have a new life in Christ?
- Have you stated that this Gospel is truly "for you" the hearer?

Sermon Preparation Worksheet

Text:_____

God Is the Actor _____

What is God doing or wanting to do through this text?

State the action of God in one sentence.

How is God presently acting in this world according to this text?

Jesus Is Our Redeemer _____

How does this text point us to Jesus for salvation?

How was the Gospel written for "you?"

How can or should the congregation see themselves in this text?

How can the sermon be preached so people believe the Gospel is for them?

The Holy Spirit Works Faith _____

When are people encouraged to believe in the works of God?

When are people encouraged to believe in God / Jesus Himself?

Are there times when the "for you" section points to tangible events? If not, how could that be strengthened?

Theme sentence_____

Sermon Preparation Worksheet: Law and Gospel

Page 1

- Identify 3-5 examples of "Law" within this biblical text.
- Note those examples that complement your theme sentence.

Page 2

- Identify similar Law examples in the present world.
- Which commandment would be broken if this Law were not kept?
- Are there times your sheep (congregation) also break this Law? Is this a law people take pleasure in breaking? Do people feel guilty when breaking this Law? Would people feel that God is angry when this Law is broken?

Page 3

- Why would Jesus become involved in saving people from this particular sin?
- How does Jesus' death and resurrection save people from this particular sin?

Page 4

- What are the ways that you see your theme sentence affecting the biblical scene?
- How is Jesus bringing Gospel to this biblical scene?
- If an Old Testament or Epistle passage, how is Christ involved in this Bible story?

Page 5

- How does your theme sentence show the Gospel in this present world?
- In what ways are you allowing the congregation believe they have a new life in Christ?
- Have you stated that this Gospel is truly "for you" the hearer?